CO DURHAM

Edited by Allison Dowse

To Grandma and Grandad
I hope you enjoy
this book.

From

Jack,

☺

First published in Great Britain in 2003 by
YOUNG WRITERS
Remus House,
Coltsfoot Drive,
Peterborough, PE2 9JX
Telephone (01733) 890066

HB ISBN 1 84460 206 0
SB ISBN 1 84460 207 9

FOREWORD

Young Writers was established in 1991 as a foundation for promoting the reading and writing of poetry amongst children and young adults. Today it continues this quest and proceeds to nurture and guide the writing talents of today's youth.

From this year's competition Young Writers is proud to present a showcase of the best poetic talent from across the UK. Each hand-picked poem has been carefully chosen from over 66,000 'Hullabaloo!' entries to be published in this, our eleventh primary school series.

This year in particular we have been wholeheartedly impressed with the quality of entries received. The thought, effort, imagination and hard work put into each poem impressed us all and once again the task of editing was a difficult but enjoyable experience.

We hope you are as pleased as we are with the final selection and that you and your family will continue to be entertained with *Hullabaloo! Co Durham* for many years to come.

CONTENTS

Lucy Alderson	1

Barnard Castle CE Primary School

Ashley Wright	1
Bethany Lowes	2
Emily Wood	2
Rebecca Walker	3
Matthew Rogers	3
Jordon Oliver	4
Vikki Lowson	5
James Raine	6
Shona Dickson	6
Michael Herbert	7
Marcus Sowerby	7
Kimberley Moore	8
Natalie Hobson	8
Martin White	9
Sara Kelly	9
William Pickworth	10
Alice Carr	10
Scott Stephenson	11
Matthew Porter	11
Vikki Thwaites	12
Richard Harding	13
Aaron Roberts	13
Catherine Bainbridge	14
Jessica Lee-Shield	14
Rebecca Watson	15
Emily Collin	15
Nicholas Wilkinson	16
Michael Harris	16
Tom Sparrow	17
Richard Teasdale	17
Amy Tones	18
Fiona Cook	18

| Lewis Gallon | 19 |
| Chloe Redpath | 19 |

Bowes Hutchinson CE Aided School

John Ettey	19
Sarah Kearton	20
Will Howard	20
Freddie Goodall	21
Ryan Haddick	21
Thomas Addison	22
Stacey McKitton	22
Rebecca Gill	23
Stephen Lawton	23
Tom Greaves	24
Catherine Spooner	24

Cockfield Primary School

Lucy Child	25
Gemma Ozap	26
Michael Teasdale	26
Ryan Slee	27
Helene Louise Petch	28
Josh Walker	28
Robert Raine	29
Bethany Nellis	30
Robyn Wilkinson	30
Lewis Pattison	31
Sophie Hope	32
Joelene Dixon	32

Croft CE Primary School

Vicky Ramsden	33
Rachel Gamble-Flint	34
Katie Wilson	34
Anna Seymour	35
Connor Christie	36
James Emmerson	36
Bethany King	37

Steven Hill   38
Jack Caulton   39

Dene House Primary School
Becky Duffy   39
Simone Laverick   40
Amy Keily   40
Faye James   41
Sean Hubery   41
Sophie Luckhurst   42
Jamie Elves   42
Sarah Tough   43
Gavin McCluskey   44
Jake Unsworth   44
Abbi Newhouse   45
Beth Clark   45
Sam Laidlaw   46
Jack Sayers   46
Heather Robinson   47
Paula Mitchell   47
Amy Moorfield   48
Liam Knox   48
James Burton   49
Jade Townley   49
Rhys Taylor   50

Dodmire Junior School
Tegan Stevenson   50
Robert Ward   51
Sarah Thompson   51
Ellie Abel   52
John Flinn   52
Thomas Taylor   53
David Lonsdale   53
Catherine Robinson   54
Andrew Lonsdale   54
Kira Bennett   55
Hannah Tinnion   55

Hayley Pritchard	56
Susan Sung	56
Jo Leonard	57
Kathryn Woolston	57
Natalie Winter	58
Jessica Duncan	58
Martin Hammond	59
Susan Glew	59
Elizabeth Doubleday	60
Justine Wears	60
Samantha McPhee	61
Charlotte Wiper	62
Shannon Mooney	62
Rebecca Hindmarch	63
Amy Bearpark	63
Nicholas Wiper	64
Paige Mooney	64

Durham Gilesgate Primary School

Rebecca Wilson	64
Stephen Mickle	65
Dean Cowan	66
Jordan Nicholson	67
Amy Foster	68
Rachael Staff	68
Stephanie Foster	69
Rebecca Mason	70
Jade Sharp	70
Reanne Finnigan	71
Cameron Dodd	71

Easington Colliery Primary School

Stacey Archer	72
Sarah Marine	72
Jonathan Turnbull	73
Gemma Middleton	73
Nathan Forster	74
Rachael Huitson	74

Sarah Naisbett	75
Jennifer Adamson	76
Sarah Heppell	76
Craig Williamson	77
Anna Constance Hewitson	78
Laura Elwell	78
Alexandra Chapman	79
Terri-Anne Cooper	79
Sarah Emerson	80
Alex Birbeck	80
Gemma Black	81
Rachel Handy	81
Carly Moore	82
Ashleigh Westmoreland	82
Faye Johnson	83
Martyn Robinson	84
Mykal Hutton	84
Stuart Muir	85
Louise Parkin	85
Connor Robson	86
David Robinson	86
Danielle Kenney	87
Anna Chapman	87
Andrew Cook	88
Amy Louise Bradley	88
Lauren Fenwick	89
Christopher Parker	89
Chelsea Price	90
Amy Wilson	90
Beccy Bradley	91
Rebecca Turnbull	92
David Green	92
Martyn Corrigan	93
Jonathon Lewins	94

Ludworth Primary School

Zoe Stones	94
Helen Atkinson	95

Scott Carter	95
Craig Whittle	96
Rachel Nadine Stabler	96
Jonathan Kell	97
Matt Keeble	97
Jonathan Sutherland	98
Kieryn Heseltine	98
Hannah Critchlow	99
Kate Critchlow	99
Stevie-Leigh Hall	100
Toni Edwards	100
Daniel Lee	101
Andrew Whittle	101

Ouston Junior School

Benjamin Brown	102
Jack Aiston	102
Lindsey Wharton	103
Abigail Forster	103
Sally Ann Rawlinson	104
Samuel Johnson	104
Philip Harland	105
Rachael Yeadon	105
Lauren Patterson	106
Katie Rebecca Hampson	106
Chelsey Brittany Parker	107
Rachel Laidler	107
Jack Thirlwell	108
Anna Drake	108
Laura McDermott	108
Ben Wilson	109
Andrew Ballantyne	109
Sophie Taylor	109
Charlotte Hogg	110
Lauren Jackson	110
Andrew Ellison	111
Benjamin Mulligan	111

Ravensworth Terrace Primary School

Michael Fella	111
Jonathan Lloyd	112
Jordan Fleming	112
Charlotte Bell	113
Leah Cosgrove	114
Christopher Cowan	114
Sara Louise Glen	115
Sophie Malay Muncaster	116
Charlotte Lynn	116
Derry Barton	117
Nicola Jane Carter	118
Carmel Woolmington	118
Lee Alcock	119
Callum Farrage	119
Connor Rogerson	120
Lauren Malloy	120
Amy O'Mara	121
Joshua Gray	121
Sean Starmer	122

Raventhorpe Preparatory School

Craig Turnbull	122
Hannah Hillary	123
Olivia Richardson	123
Victoria Richardson	124
Victoria Whitaker	124
Samantha Hopper	125
Simon Warne	125
Adam Matthews	126
Danielle Connelly	126
Jamie Kilday	127
Jonathan Sayer	127
Georgina Williamson	128
Jessica Harland	128
Amy Matthews	129
Billie-Rae Wilkerson	130
Debbie Cheesbrough	130

Cheryl Gartland 131
Jessica Rushforth 131
Harriet Peacock 132

St Augustine's Primary School, Darlington
Thomas Caygill 132
Natasha Redpath 133
Matthew Morgan 134
Ciar Purser 134
Lisa Thornton 134
Jonathan Lumsdon 135
Emma Spraggon 135
Helen Richardson 136
Bianca Fawlk 136
Leo Logan Cassidy 137
Joss Klein 137
Katharine Murphy 138
Andrew Wynne 138
Hayley Eccles 139
Robert Corless 139
Danny Smith 139
Emma Mitchell 140
Sean Simpson 140
Emma Galbraith 141
David McGovern 141

St Cuthbert's RC Primary School, Crook
Anna Barnes 142
Philipa Donaghue 142
Natalie Poulter 143

St Joseph's RC Primary School, Durham
Bridget Harrison 143
Thuy Pham Thi Minh 144
Ben Newton 144
Joe Hoban 145
Liam Scollen 145
Laura Scotter 146

Georgia Lincoln   146
Mark Hunter   147
Richard Misiak   147
Joseph Hirst   148
David Hopper   148
Caitlin Scullion   149

St Teresa's RC Primary School, Darlington
Jade Pearson   149
Thomas Bell   150
Ryan Thorns   150
Joe Hewitt   150
James Smith   151
Thomas Manning   151
Christopher Thomas Ward   151
Michael Holmes   152
Jack Doherty   152
Rachel Bell   152
Megan McSherry & Aisha Shariff   153
Gabrielle McKenna   153
Michael Thurloway   154
Kieran Elliot   154
Jessica Addison   155
Ashleigh Moss   155
Charlotte Foster   156
Stuart Watson   156
Rebecca Bates   156
Mark James Anderson   157
Mandeep Uppal   157
Lauren Wilthew   158
Abbi Sheriff   158
Haydn McKenna   158
Ryan Kindred   159
Amanda Walker   159

St Wilfrid's RC VA Primary School, Bishop Auckland
Jade Watson   160
Philip Johnson   160

Keiron Tague   161
Jonathon Wright   161
Shelby Ballan   162
Emma Quinn   162
Inkie Ralph   163
Lewis Wright   163
Katie Burge   164
Abby Whitworth   164
Brogan Donnelly   165
Anna Bentley   166
Patrick Hoban   166
Adam Oyston   167
Hayley McClory   167
Lucy Watson   168
Amy Watson   168
Bethany Kelly   169
Kieran McCormick   169
Keiran Whigham   169
Paige Tully   170
Domonic Bylett   170
Olyvia Fairless   171

Staindrop CE Primary School

Niall Cronin   171
Dale Gilbert   172
Mark Anthony Humble   172
Matthew Sugden   173
Ross Lindsay   173
Cara Firmin   174
Samuel Fells   175
Claire Boyes   176
Amy Heritage   176
Matthew Thompson   177
Kirsty Davies   177
Christopher Pearson   178
Michael Boyes   178
Sarah Thompson   179
Hayd'n Walker   179

Peter Bousfield	180
Nathan Nicholson	180
Josh Wade	181
Philippa Smith	182
Adam Cansfield	182
Ashleigh Hewitt	183
Jenny Kirby	183

Stanley (Crook) Primary School

Daniel Grainger	183
Chelsea Edmundson	184
Amy Martin	184
Dean Moore	184
Rachael Littlewood	184
Laura Simpson	185
Sara Bell	186
Flora McCabe	186
Adam Alderson	186

Shotton Hall Junior School

Andrew Bell	187
Scott Mills	187
Robyn Pallister	188
Ross Atkinson	188
Mathew Geldard	189
Jonathan Scholick	189
Andrew Westgarth	190
Gemma Scott	190
Michelle Burey	191
Liam Swift	191
Sophie Coldwell	192
Scott Westmorland	192
Liam Wheatley	192
Lee Cuthbert	193
Jennifer Legg	193
Kate Fletcher	194

The Poems

LILIES

Ladies dancing
Their white gowns flow,
In the garden
Where the lilies grow.
Whirling faster,
When a gust of wind blows,
The lilies are the ladies
Putting on their dancing show.

Lucy Alderson (12)

WHAT ABOUT ME?

What about me when you leave?
What about me when your mind thinks *violence?*
What about me when situations change?
What about me when you leave without me?
What about me when no one's there for me?
What about me?

What would happen to me if no one cared?
What would happen to me if disaster struck?
What would happen to me if I couldn't stop you?
What would happen to me if there were no one around?
What would happen to me if I became ill?
What would happen to me?

What should I do when I can't stop your anger?
What should I do when I can't help you through things?
What should I do when your mind goes crazy?
What should I do when I need things to live from?
What should I do when questions need answers?
What should I do?
Who will be there?

Ashley Wright (10)
Barnard Castle CE Primary School

CELEBRATIONS

C rying out, laughing, rejoice,
E vening falls, the party goes on,
L ively dancing the night away,
E ating buns and chocolate cake,
B irthdays, Christmas, Easter too,
R elieved when it's time for bed, I'm so tired,
A ching feet and throbbing hands,
T ea, coffee, wine and beer are bursting full of celebration cheer,
I 'm stuffed, I can't eat another bite, well, maybe just maybe,
   a slice of cake,
O ff to the land of dreams for me, I hope,
N ow it's Monday, we're back at school, I can't wait for next time!

Bethany Lowes (10)
Barnard Castle CE Primary School

UNBELIEVABLE SENSES

I saw a grown man wear a pink dress.
I heard the baby say grown-up words.
I smelt the sweetness of magic.
I tasted the root of the table and chair.
I smelt the lovingness of a romantic couple.

I saw a bottle of water turn blood-red.
I heard the sound of fear.
I smelt the bee's sting.
I tasted the white, fluffy clouds.
I felt the coldness of summer.

Emily Wood (11)
Barnard Castle CE Primary School

DREAMS

D rifting off in a peaceful dream,
R owing to a distant island,
E verything is controlled by me, the dreamer,
A live . . . partly,
M y feelings no longer matter to me,
S o sweet are my dreams and I hope they never end.

D ay dreams and night dreams,
R ocketing through the sky,
E ars popping, prickling,
A whizzing comet and stars glittering,
M y heart is fluttering,
S pace dreams are beautiful.

Rebecca Walker (11)
Barnard Castle CE Primary School

INCREDIBLE SENSES

I smelt the rumbling sound of a volcano.
I heard the seagull laugh.
I saw the man being walked by a mouse.
I tasted the rust of an old iron bar.
I felt the far corner of space.

I smelt the sweetness of magic.
I heard the sound of greed.
I tasted the rot of an old wooden chair.
I saw the curtains slowly start to close.
I felt boiling hot molten lava from a volcano.

Matthew Rogers (11)
Barnard Castle CE Primary School

DIARY FROM SCHOOL

Monday; on Monday the teacher droned on about art,
I amused myself by pulling a paintbrush apart.
Got sent to the head,
A letter went home and when I arrived, got sent to bed.

Tuesday; on Tuesday things got a bit better,
But then at play, I got stung by a bee.
Year 5s laughed when I did cry,
The school nurse kept on shouting, 'It's OK, you won't die.'

Wednesday; on Wednesday things didn't get any better,
Forgot my homework, so went the letter,
I got home and my mum did shout,
I said I was sorry but she was in doubt.

Thursday; on Thursday things got even worse,
I lost some money from my purse,
(Not enough for the bus) I got a taxi, but still late,
When I got to school, the head was at the gate.

Friday; on Friday things were great,
Apart from being locked out at the school gate,
Other than my detention, my teacher went nuts,
Followed by a few hundred tuts.

The weekend went by,
I hoped and prayed,
That on Monday morning,
I would not wake up as me anymore.

Jordon Oliver (10)
Barnard Castle CE Primary School

MRS KINDERBURG

Mrs Kinderburg is the kid's favourite,
But a nightmare for my mum, Sally Cavet,
Tooth decay, chocolates, sweets, the lot!
But unfortunately our mums have an evil plot,
They'll scream and shout, 'Get out of my way!'
Just because she gives us sweets every day.
Mrs Kinderburg thinks our mums are *crazy*
And our mums think she's extremely *lazy.*

All the kids will come to her,
As she makes a homework excuse to the teacher!
We will tell our mums, 'We're off to school.'
But really we're at Mrs Kinderburg's, 'cause she's cool!
The mums are just jealous we love her best!
But when we come home now we can't get a rest!
'Where have you been? Up at Mrs what's her name's? Playing games?'
I just want to scream 'Yes!'
Because I love my mum less!

Mrs Kinderburg gave me a crumpet today,
But my mum took me out to play!
She gave me pancakes and a bike!
I think Mrs Kinderburg took a hike!
I love my mum more really,
But sometimes she gets on my nerves,
I think I like her best now,
Unless Mrs Kinderburg returns.

Vikki Lowson (11)
Barnard Castle CE Primary School

PLAYGROUND

Some people are chewing some gum,
Some people are doing some work,
Some people are chasing the boys,
Some people are running from girls,
Some people are chatting to teachers,
Some people are catching Year 3s.

Some boys are playing with footballs,
Some boys are singing a song,
Some boys are running from girls,
Some boys are chatting up girls,
Some boys are hiding inside,
Some boys are catching Year 3s.

Some girls are messing about,
Some girls are singing a song,
Some girls are getting dressed up,
Some girls are chasing the boys,
Some girls are chatting up boys,
Some girls are playing a game.

Some people never change, it's play time again.

James Raine (10)
Barnard Castle CE Primary School

DREAMS

D   reaming can be fun,
R   emembering them is hard,
E   yes get heavy,
A   way you drift,
M   ust go to sleep,
S   ilently drifting away.

Shona Dickson (10)
Barnard Castle CE Primary School

DREAM

Drifting, gliding, flying through,
I love sliding in the blue.
Nothing to stop me, nothing at all,
Then suddenly I begin to fall.

Crashing, zooming, going down,
I hit the floor and crack my crown.
I feel all dizzy, flying around,
My heart then starts to pound.

Where am I? Where am I?
I must stand up and fly,
The air whips my face and I begin to cry.
'Oh please, the last thing I want to do is die!'

Finally I begin to wake again,
My head in such terrible pain.
'It's all a dream,' I say to myself,
It's all a dream.

Michael Herbert (11)
Barnard Castle CE Primary School

TELL ME LITTLE WOODWORM

Tell me little woodworm
Wriggling on your belly,
Why not come inside
And see what's on the telly?
Goodness gracious little woodworm
You've eaten all the chairs,
That's why poor little Marcus
Is sitting on the stairs!

Marcus Sowerby (8)
Barnard Castle CE Primary School

ARTHUR CROCKIT

Arthur Crockit, Arthur Crockit,
He went to school with gum in his pocket,
He went to English
And made a wish,
He spoke to Sue
And his wish came true.
He had for lunch, slices of pizza
And afterwards, went and blew up the teacher.
Arthur Crockit, Arthur Crockit,
He had a straw in his pocket,
He raised it up,
He blew and blew
And the paper flew,
It landed on top of a third year's head,
He heard the teacher, he will soon be dead.
He tried to run but ran into the teacher,
He surely wished she was a Christian preacher.
Arthur Crockit, Arthur Crockit,
Next time he'll go to school with empty pockets.

Kimberley Moore (10)
Barnard Castle CE Primary School

FIONA!

Fiona is my friend -
Is kind,
Fiona is my pal -
Is helpful,
Fiona is my partner -
Is a great friend,
Fiona!

Natalie Hobson (8)
Barnard Castle CE Primary School

SCHOOL ASSEMBLY

On Monday he talked about aluminium cans,
but all I could find was some rubber bands.

On Tuesday he talked about people who are blind,
but I know to them I'm always kind.

On Wednesday he talked about how to eat food
and what to do when you have chewed.

On Thursday he talked about writing a story,
no wonder the Celts never got their glory.

On Friday he talked about who won the football,
who hit the ref and made him fall.

On Saturday and Sunday, peace after all,
until my mum got an important phone call.

Martin White (11)
Barnard Castle CE Primary School

MY BEST FRIEND

My best friend is big and tall
My other best friend is very small
My third best friend is always awake
My fourth best friend is never late
My fifth best friend is never shy
My sixth best friend does never lie
My seventh best friend loves lemonade
My eighth best friend likes orange maids
My ninth best friend is always kind
My tenth best friend is hard to find.

Sara Kelly (8)
Barnard Castle CE Primary School

WEIRD SENSES

I saw the sun cough up snow.
I smelt the sound of a little girl's bow.
I felt the bitterness of a friendly storm.
I tasted the sound of a spider being born.

I saw a tree lick itself clean.
I smelt the sound of a book being mean.
I felt the bitterness of a summer sun.
I tasted the sound of a laser gun.

I saw an elephant spell 'onomatopoeia'.
I smelt the sound of a deaf man hear.
I felt the bitterness of a sweet warm bath.
I tasted the sound of an evil giraffe.

William Pickworth (11)
Barnard Castle CE Primary School

LOVE CYCLE

Becky fancies Jake,
Who pines for Iona,
Who's always chasing Daniel around,
Who gives all his love to Eleanor,
Who simply adores Lewis,
To whom Chloe is a heroine in his eyes,
Who wastes away for Adam,
Who gazes at Jessica
And it's Aaron she aches for,
Who lolls around at Becky
And it all begins again!

Alice Carr (8)
Barnard Castle CE Primary School

IMPOSSIBLE SENSES

I saw a lake freeze in an instant,
I heard a fish cry of sorrow,
I felt all the colours of the rainbow,
I smelt the sweetness of the wizard's spell,
I tasted the white fluffy cloud.

I saw an oak tree creep from side to side,
I heard a bird laugh its head off,
I felt the song go to my head,
I smelt the leaves fall from a tree,
I tasted the colour of the mouldy sprout.

I saw the sky drop and hover,
I saw an elephant touch a mouse,
I saw some lava freeze itself,
I saw a mountain move for a goat,
I saw a picture weep a river.

Scott Stephenson (11)
Barnard Castle CE Primary School

PEOPLE'S FEELINGS

Some people feel happy
Others feel sad
Just like my dad
Some people feel helpful, some feel lazy
Some people feel tough and strong
Some feel weak and pointless on this planet
Some people feel brave
Some feel scared and cold
But I feel just right as I am.

Matthew Porter (8)
Barnard Castle CE Primary School

SCHOOLDAYS

On Monday the teacher talked of art,
I felt as if I were falling apart.
The teacher told me I was very rude,
He sent me out in an awful mood.
On Tuesday he told us of the playground mud,
I do really think I misunderstood.
I was so bored, I blew a bubble,
I got into great big trouble.
On Wednesday it got even worse,
It felt like I had some kind of curse.
I saw everyone see me pick my nose,
Up came the head, it ruined the day.
On Thursday he talked of kindness and grace,
I thought this a total disgrace.
I then started to talk and chatter,
The head came up and started to shout and natter.
On Friday he said of giving favours,
This wouldn't work with my behaviour.
I stretched my arms and gave a yawn,
The teacher screeched, 'Are you so bored!'
The weekend at last,
The week has passed.
It was then I got on my knees to pray,
'Please God, let me be good on Monday!'

Vikki Thwaites (10)
Barnard Castle CE Primary School

SENSES IMPOSSIBLE

I have seen a cat swim,
I have heard a bird bark,
I have smelt a rhino's blood,
I have tasted a lifework,
I have touched a volcano's heat.

I have seen a clock chime thirteen,
I heard the sound of death,
I have smelt new life,
I have tasted the sweat of a jaguar,
I have touched the Colossus of Rhodes.

I have seen the whole world from a tower,
I have heard the colour's harmony,
I have smelt a dream,
I have tasted the desert's centre,
I have touched the eye of an elephant.

Richard Harding (11)
Barnard Castle CE Primary School

YOU!

You! Are small, smaller than Marcus!
You! Are a good pal!
You! Your eyes are green and brown.
You! Live in Dawson Road.
You! Your hair is blonde turning brown.
You! Are my pal, my pal Lewis Quinn.

Aaron Roberts
Barnard Castle CE Primary School

IMPOSSIBLE SENSES

I saw the sky flicker multicoloured.
I heard the sun shout at the sky,
I felt a snowman squeeze my hand,
I tasted a piece of rotten wood,
I smelt the roots of an old oak tree.

I saw my mum cry purple tears,
I heard a butterfly's heart beat,
I felt the moon as I went past in a plane,
I tasted the sweetness of the rainbow,
I smelt the skeleton of a live kitten.

I saw the rainbow switch its colours,
I heard an ant weep huge tears,
I felt the insides of a stripy elephant,
I tasted an ancient piece of paper,
I smelt the joy of a great big snake.

Catherine Bainbridge (10)
Barnard Castle CE Primary School

MY PETS

I have some pets around my house,
But none would try to catch a mouse.
One of my pets has big teeth and is fluffy white,
It eats lots of carrots so it can see at night.

One of my pets is fluffy and brown,
He says *bow wow* and always lies down.

The last of my pets lives all alone,
It swims round and round in a big glass bowl.

Jessica Lee-Shield (8)
Barnard Castle CE Primary School

SUNBEAMS

Sunbeams blazing from the warm sun,
Sunbeams glistening at the window,
Sunbeams reflecting on a blue sea,
Sunbeams are hot and yellow,
Sunbeamed sunbeams.

Sunbeams glimmering over this land,
Sunbeams like red-hot lava are
Falling, falling to the scorching ground,
Sunblinds are lowering,
When sunbeams are hovering, hovering.

Sunbeams are sparkling like the moon,
Sparkling, sparkling like sparks,
Sunbeams warm and red-hot,
Sunbeams glaring at you,
Summer, sunbeamed sky.

Rebecca Watson (8)
Barnard Castle CE Primary School

IN THE PLAYGROUND

Monday I played skipping and got chased by the boys that were hitting.
Tuesday I played ball and I ended up chucking it over the wall.
Wednesday I played 'tig' and accidentally pulled off the teacher's wig.
Thursday I played 'stuck in the mud' and I really did get stuck
in the mud.
Friday I played 'push off the bench' and I broke my leg.
Saturday I was in hospital and I fell off the bed.
Sunday I was a total wreck!

Emily Collin (10)
Barnard Castle CE Primary School

MAKING CHOICES

I wake - see a bright light
Look around - see all white
Nurses, doctors, cold sharp needle;
I see my mum,
Coldness in my arm.
I see my dad - going, going . . .
My eyelids get heavier, heavier, heaver . . .

I see Mum stop, head in hands,
Dad sits, holding his hands over his face;
I try to move my head - I can't
I try to move my hands - I can't
I look around
More doctors, nurses - white
I cry, 'Mum, Dad.' They rush to me . . .

I tell them of the lights.

Nicholas Wilkinson (10)
Barnard Castle CE Primary School

YOU

You! You are very small
You! Your eyes are as brown as a snail's shell
You! Your eyes are like a racing track
You! Your mouth is red as a rose
You! Your head is round like a ball
You! You're my friend.

Michael Harris
Barnard Castle CE Primary School

PLANE JOURNEY

I sat up; more bored than ever,
Wondering if the journey would end,
But for me it felt like never.
'Mum, how long to go?' I asked.
Mum made no reply with her coffee and flask.
It surely must be landing time now, I thought.
I sat there bored and feeling distraught,
But all of a sudden, I felt a thud,
I don't know what it was, but it felt good.
We went really fast and then slowed down
And finally came to a stop.
I got out of my seat and jumped around and around
And my aching ears went *pop!*

Tom Sparrow (11)
Barnard Castle CE Primary School

ART

Inspiring, enjoyable,
Fun, impressive,
Funky, fantastic,
Colourful, bright,
Dull, brilliant,
Great, wonderful,
Bizarre, oil paints,
Water paints, poster paints,
Art!

Richard Teasdale (11)
Barnard Castle CE Primary School

You!

You!
Your hair is like brown chocolate melting in the hot sun
You!
Your eyes are like brown pebbles in the soft sand
You!
Your hands are like pink sausages in a pan
You!
Your ears are like pink flowers on a green stem
You!
Your feet are like chair legs on a stool
You!
Your nose is like a cute pink pig snout on a piglet
You!
Your name is Hayley!

Amy Tones (8)
Barnard Castle CE Primary School

You!

You love water!
You!
You are big and shiny,
You!
You live in the deep blue ocean,
You!
You are black and white, a killer,
You!
You're a whale - as big as a house.

Fiona Cook (8)
Barnard Castle CE Primary School

AMY TONES

You! You make me feel comfortable
You! Your eyes are as colourful as the sea
You! Your hair is like sand
You! Your ears are like leopard's skin
You! Your friendship is normal.

Lewis Gallon
Barnard Castle CE Primary School

YOU!

You! Your eyes are as blue as the sea, never-ending
You! Your nose is like a big rose, always smelling
You! Your ears are like a mouse hole, always listening
You! Your hands are like small hedgehogs, always burrowing
You! Your clothes are like smelly pigs, never changing.

Chloe Redpath (8)
Barnard Castle CE Primary School

WATERFALLS

The waterfall throws
Barrels of water into the
Rippling dark lake beneath.

The waterfall never tires and
Never stops unless there is a
Drought.

John Ettey (10)
Bowes Hutchinson CE Aided School

EASY PEASY

You want me to ride a bike upside down
And write it in the Guinness Book of World Records
At the same time?
Easy peasy!

You want me to eat a pear
And catch a hare?
Easy peasy!

You want me to blow up 100
Balloons in 10 seconds?
Easy peasy!

You want me to run a mile
In 7 seconds?
Easy peasy!

You want me to eat the cream off
The top of some milk?
Impossible!

Sarah Kearton (10)
Bowes Hutchinson CE Aided School

WILEY WIFRONTS' Y-FRONTS

Wiley Wifronts bought some Y-fronts
The Y-fronts were wider than Wiley thought
Wiley Wifronts' wide Y-fronts were so wide
Wiley wondered, *Wiley, you ought not to have*
Bought Y-fronts so wide.

Will Howard (11)
Bowes Hutchinson CE Aided School

I BELIEVE

I believe that there won't be a war
And everyone will get along

I believe that people one day
Will get a job and more food and drink

I believe that
We can live without racism

I believe that refugees will live safely
In their right country

I hope that we can
Live together and play together

If I didn't believe
Nobody would read this
And these things could happen

I know that there are more people
Who are more important than others
There are some people without a roof over them.

Believe me.

Freddie Goodall (10)
Bowes Hutchinson CE Aided School

SUSAN SMELLS' SMELLY SOCKS

Susan Smells said she could smell her smelly socks,
So Susan Smells smelt smelly socks,
Susan Smells splashed her smelly socks into the soaking water,
Now Susan Smells' smelly socks aren't smelly anymore.

Ryan Haddick (9)
Bowes Hutchinson CE Aided School

THAT'S PIMPS

You want me to make a million
Hammers in ten seconds?
That's pimps.
You want me to lift Mount Everest
With my little finger
And juggle singers?
That's pimps.
You want me to throw the world
Into deep space
And scamper back?
That's pimps.
But,
Eating my mum's Yorkshire puddings
Is the hardest thing in the world,
Believe me.

Thomas Addison (10)
Bowes Hutchinson CE Aided School

THE SUN

The sun is like a bowling ball,
High up in the sky.
The sun is an orange or a face in disguise.
The sun is like a bouncy ball,
Bouncing in the air.
The sun is like a light
That shines upon us
And what would we do if
It was not there?

Stacey McKitton (11)
Bowes Hutchinson CE Aided School

I BELIEVE

I believe
That everyone
Should have happy lives
And enough food
To feed their families

I believe
That everyone
Should have a good home
To live in and spend their lives in

I believe
There should be
No wars
It doesn't do anyone any good

I believe.

Rebecca Gill (10)
Bowes Hutchinson CE Aided School

EGG

There was a man in Bowes
Who began to beg,
I had no money
So I gave him an egg.

The egg it put a smile upon his face,
'Thank you,' he said.
I looked at his face
And he walked with me
At a brilliant pace.

Stephen Lawton (10)
Bowes Hutchinson CE Aided School

MOULDY MOLLY'S MANKY MOLES

Mouldy Molly grew manky moles,
Mouldy Molly's manky moles
Grew mankier more and more,
Mouldy Molly's manky moles
Grew more than Molly meant,
Mouldy Molly's manky moles
Were so manky,
Mouldy Molly's manky mum
Made Mouldy Molly mad,
Mouldy Molly's manky mum said,
'Molly, your moles are minging!'

Tom Greaves (11)
Bowes Hutchinson CE Aided School

I BELIEVE

I believe that people
Are really kind to other people

I believe that people
Will be friends forever

I believe that people
Will share things

I believe that people
Say please and thank you for things.

Catherine Spooner (11)
Bowes Hutchinson CE Aided School

THE MORNING SNOW

The housetops were covered,
The garden was bare,
As I woke up,
I had to stare.

There was snow all around,
It was a sight,
To see my friends,
Having a snowball fight.

I shouted, 'Whoopee!'
I shouted, 'Hooray!'
What a perfect start
To a wonderful day.

I hurried downstairs,
Nearly knocked over my mother,
Had some toast
And ran into my brother.

My brother he stood,
As tall as tall,
He went outside
And threw a snowball.

It hit my dog,
Floss gave a yelp,
I got dressed upstairs
And went down to help.

Lucy Child (11)
Cockfield Primary School

MY SNOWY MORNING

When I got up this morning,
What a beautiful sight I saw,
A white glittering blanket of snow I saw.

I jumped out of my pyjamas,
Put on my clothes
And ran down my stairs.

I opened my front door,
I shouted, 'Hooray, hooray,
No school, no school today!'

Then there goes the telephone,
Ring, ring, ring, ring.
I answered, it was my teacher,
'There's no school today.'

I jumped in the air before
My teacher could say,
'No school for the rest of the week I am afraid.'

Gemma Ozap (10)
Cockfield Primary School

SNOWY MORNING

When I opened my bedroom curtains, what a sight,
There was a lot of snow and it was white, white, white.
Oh golly, oh gosh, what a sight I saw,
I shouted, 'I want more, more, more.'
When I went downstairs I said, 'Look, look at the snow.'
My mum and dad said, 'We know, we know.'
I put on my clothes in a rush,

I said, 'It better not turn to slush
And it better not melt.'
As my dad puts on his belt,
'School better be off,'
I said with a cough.
My mum said, 'Sadly it's not,
But there is still a lot of snow, a lot, a lot.'

Michael Teasdale (11)
Cockfield Primary School

THE SNOWY MAN

When he begins to cry,
The snowflakes trickle from his eye,
When the blizzard begins to brew,
The only sounds are the cows moaning moo.
When the snowstorm begins to fall,
The children are making a huge snowball.

When he enters his home, what a sight, 'It's a dome.'
He makes his way in the house
And what does he see? A field mouse.
He soon goes to bed that night
And gets a frost-bitten bite.

He opens the curtain and what a sight,
He's sure to get a fright,
For the snow is two or three inches tall,
But now a snowfall,
Before he goes in the shed,
He better go back to bed.

Ryan Slee (11)
Cockfield Primary School

A BLANKET OF SNOW

On the first sight of snow,
What a chill met my toe,
I rushed out to see the sight,
Of miles around sparkling white -

Whirls and twirls,
Circles around the chestnut tree,
As it's formed,
Drifts and blizzards,
Glitter around,
As the snow angels came -
I went to get my hat, scarves and gloves.

By the end of the day -
My toes were cold,
I went to bed,
With the snow outside of me.

That was all of the snowy day.

Helene Louise Petch (10)
Cockfield Primary School

THE SNOW MONSTER

Early morning he is there,
Children come to stand and stare.
In their coats, hats and gloves,
All stood there like a flock of doves.

All of a sudden there was a great cry
And the snow monster sneezed and said, 'Where am I?'
He started to shout, he started to bellow,
For all of a sudden he was turning yellow!

He said, 'Oh no, I'm starting to melt,
Soon I'll be as soft as felt.
I will start to drip and soon I will die.'
And he sank into the soil with a big sigh.

Josh Walker (11)
Cockfield Primary School

SNOW

Snow, snow
O glory snow
See how it grows
In the country the sight -
Is white

The morning comes
And children come out
They have snowball fights
And shout about
The snowmen built
The ice is chilled

It cracks and snaps
Brittle as can be
People shout, 'Yippee!'
The cars skid and slide
Some even collide

At the end of the day
Some stay
Some go
People go
Hoping for more
Snow!

Robert Raine (10)
Cockfield Primary School

A SNOWY MORNING

Silvery-white snow glistened in the night,
While I was sleeping in a nice comfy bed,
When I got up, I opened the curtains,
I got a big shock.
When I was going to school
The snow was crackling between my cold, wet feet,
Also the sun was keeping my face warm,
When I got to school it was covered in a wet, white, silvery blanket
With bits of slush in it,
The snow will be melting into little bits of crackling snow
In-between the gaps in the houses,
I need to be careful - as I go
In case a big snowflake might go down my face.
Now the sun is out,
It will be melting down the street,
Saying goodbye.

Bethany Nellis (10)
Cockfield Primary School

FROST FRIGHT!

As I drew back the curtains,
I saw a white haven
And a girl in the snow,
Vigorously waving!

The garden was covered
And all very white,
But one thing intruded,
Growing in height!

It had a black eye
And another,
But then I saw
My best friend's brother!

He wore a scarf
And a pompomed hat,
With polka dot stripes,
On the snow he sat!

Robyn Wilkinson (10)
Cockfield Primary School

SNOWY POEM

As I opened my curtains this morning
What a sight met my eyes
On the floor and cars was a blanket of snow
So I went to my nan, 'It has been snowing!'
You could hear children laughing with excitement
It was like they had never seen snow before
I went downstairs and got dressed
I had my breakfast, then I got my bag
I got my coat then I said, 'I am going to school.'
'Alright,' shouted Nan
So I went to school
I hoped it would be off
It was not off
So I went into the schoolyard
And had a snowball fight with my friends.

Lewis Pattison (11)
Cockfield Primary School

THE SNOW HAS COVERED THE COUNTRY TODAY!

Icicles, footprints, snowmen - hooray!
The snow has covered the country today!
The glistening white snow - out there it lay
And in barns, in fields - it has covered the hay.

Icicles hanging from the houses' rooftops
And in most of the schools, the boilers go *pop!*
The children in wellies, trousers tucked in
And the snowplough's sharp blade which is made out of tin.

Soon it would be gone, soon it would melt,
I was down to the last snowflake, the last one I felt.
I hope it will happen again next winter,
I'm not even bothered if it's only a splinter!

Goodbye snow!

Sophie Hope (10)
Cockfield Primary School

A SNOWFALL

Glittery snow glistened in the night
All of the snow carefully falling
On the glittery cars
On the way to school
Children throwing snowballs around -
Kids falling over on the ground -
Kids running in the slush
The snow crackling in-between my feet -
I wished that school would be cancelled
Very sadly school was on.

Joelene Dixon (11)
Cockfield Primary School

SNOW

Clouds swoop so low you can almost touch them,
A secret mist covers the grey moist sky,
Snowflakes fall like dancing fairies,
Racing silently to the ground forming a glistening carpet of snow.

At the bottom of the garden stands a lady frozen in her beauty,
Her gown trailing behind her.
Bare skeletons wear ripped layers of frost
And shiver as the gale howls through every bone in their bodies.

Lifeless waterfalls freeze in their motion,
Frozen streams are slithering snakes twisting and turning.

A crystal carpet covers the undisturbed landscape,
Until snowballs whiz through the air.
Rosy cheeks glisten in the cold,
Sledge tracks scattered everywhere,
Footprints cover the ground
And children slide down mountains of snow.

Time to go!
Moans and groans of disbelief.
Now peace.
A lonely person stands,
Empty footprints surround him.

Vicky Ramsden (11)
Croft CE Primary School

Snow

The sky darkens menacingly,
Ready to release the year's first snow.
The shadows lengthen in the growing darkness,
Forbiddingly.

The first snowflakes break through the barrier of clouds
And drift down to Earth silently, twisting and dancing,
Spiralling and floating.

A giant duvet of snow,
Glitters in the morning light,
Like a silver cloak enveloping the land.

Rivers are transformed into silvery snakes,
Twisting and turning out of sight.
Waterfalls freeze into ice sculptures,
Glistening beautifully.

Trees are turned into ice-encrusted skeletons,
Or fine ladies with trailing gowns of ice.

Snowdrifts mount up against the walls,
As sheep huddle together shivering with cold.

Rachel Gamble-Flint (11)
Croft CE Primary School

Snow

A grey overcast sky hung above the frozen ground,
Snowflakes fell dancing and floating,
Drifting silently against the garden wall,
When I pulled my curtains back
A sparkling, glistening carpet of snow covered the ground,
Rivers turned to silvery snakes,
Icicles hung from rooftops like daggers,

Loud ecstatic children ran out to play,
All wrapped up nice and warm,
Snowballs glided across the sky,
Snowmen stood silently on the ground,
Sledge tracks zigzagged across the snow,
Rosy-cheeked children returned wet through.

Katie Wilson (9)
Croft CE Primary School

Snow

Overcast sky threatening to burst
Is a human mouth withholding air?
Soundlessly he lets go at last,
Snowflakes dance joyfully,
Gracefully they envelop the Earth
Like icing forming on a cake.

A hostile wind moans,
As it runs through the bare bones of the skeletal tree,
Which shivers in its skimpy garment of frost,
Waterfalls turn into ice sculptures
As the freezing ice sets.

Children shout breathlessly,
As sleighs swoop down mounds of snow,
Snowballs cascade from frosty gloves,
Soaring through the air.
Frosty trees smile cheerfully,
As ecstatic children rush around them.
Little untouched snow is left,
As zigzagging lines take over the land.

Anna Seymour (10)
Croft CE Primary School

SNOW

A grey overcast sky
Threatens the Earth
Unleashing twisting, twirling snowflakes,
Which sparkle in the moonlit sky.
As I draw back the curtains,
A glistening carpet of snow
Lays silently on the ground,
As bare trees shiver in the Arctic wind
And the distant mountains are covered
With gleaming white snow,
Children sprint out,
Snowballs collide in mid-air,
Sleighs skid down hills,
Wiggling left and right,
Under the thick woolly hats
Children shiver and splutter out
Their frosty breath.
Cries erupt out from children
When their mums say,
'It's time to come in!'

Connor Christie (10)
Croft CE Primary School

SNOW

Misty, grey, menacing clouds loom ready to release their grip.
They're falling!
Snowflakes twirling, spiralling, gliding,
Resting gently on the white sheet of snow.
Pointed icicles and frosty sculptures,
Naked trees as bare as skeletons.
A shimmering white-gowned lady walks,
Sparkling everything she touches.

Children play cheerfully,
Throwing snowballs at each other.
With numb hands and rosy cheeks,
They start to build a snowman.
The evening is quiet.
Sledge tracks zigzag down the hill
And the remains of snowmen stand in the ground.

James Emmerson (9)
Croft CE Primary School

SNOW

When I looked up in the sky
I saw
A threatening and cloudy person
About to cry frozen teardrops.
Then . . . as if it could bear it no longer,
He burst and scattered soundless white angels.
Twirling and floating they lay down like
A silver cloak upon the frozen, icy ground.
Skeleton-like ladies wearing only shimmering,
Silver gowns of snow,
Shook in the icy breeze.

Icicles hang from the roofs,
Like elephants' tusks,
The crystal mountains shimmer in the snowy valley.
I watch as all the cheerful children,
Run out and start building snowmen.
My sledge stands untouched in the hallway until . . .
Jack Frost makes another winter wonderland.

Bethany King (11)
Croft CE Primary School

SNOW

The overcast sky threatened the land
With snowflakes in its pouch.
The clouds exploded sending silver fairies gracefully
Gliding down to Earth.
The ice glistened in the sun's ray,
Like a silver snake.

Mountains of snow dominated
The Earth below.
Tiny footprints zigzagged untouched
Across the snow,
The trees, like silver ladies, wore
Gowns of sparkling diamonds.

The undisturbed carpet of snow
Lay there until
The ecstatic children burst out
Like a herd of buffalos.
Snowballs soared from side to side,
Rosy-cheeked children trudged through the snow,
Mums called out to their children,
They shivered inside
And the land was silent once more.

Steven Hill (10)
Croft CE Primary School

SNOW

The cloudy grey sky, dark and threatening
Snowflakes twirled as they drifted to the frosty ground
Leaving a carpet of glistening snow

Mountains of snow in the distance
Rivers as icy as silvery snakes
Tiny birds' footprints buried in the snow

Skeleton-like trees hanging over icy rivers

Waterfalls frozen into icy sculptures

Excited children sprint out with their sledges
Making zigzags across the snow
Snowballs gliding in mid-air

Children wrapped up in gloves and hats
Breathing out their frosty breath
Rolling a ball into a snowman
Then going in for tea.

Jack Caulton (9)
Croft CE Primary School

MY ROOM

With dirty clothes in heaps on the floor
And pop star posters stuck up on the door
Of Eminem, Will and Gareth Gates
And groovy pictures of me and my mates!
A wardrobe with my clothes neat inside,
A warm double bed in which to hide.
My mum's always nagging - she's a real pest!
But personally, I think my room is the best!

Becky Duffy (11)
Dene House Primary School

SUPERSTAR

I dreamed to be a superstar,
To travel the world in a fancy car.
To sing my songs in other lands,
Surrounded by a group of crazy fans.

I'd love to go on stage and sing,
Show off my new gold diamond ring.
Wearing super, designer clothes,
Invited to lots of celebrity shows.

All my dreams have now come true,
Now I'm happy - never blue!
Travelling the world in my fancy car,
Now, I am a superstar!

Simone Laverick (11)
Dene House Primary School

MY ROOM

Messy room, messy room,
It looks like it's been in a *boom!*
The clothes, the sweets,
I've got to get it complete.

Messy room, messy room,
How I hated that big room,
I think my room is a mess,
Messier than all the rest.

Amy Keily (11)
Dene House Primary School

THE FAIRGROUND

I woke up very early,
Turned on the lamp which was very pearly.
I waited till light begun,
I was going to have some fun!

I followed Mum down the stairs,
I followed her with my cuddly teddy bears.
My mum and I changed into our clothes,
Nearly time to set off for the shows!

My little sister sneezed, *achoo!*
It was a shame she had the flu.
My sister wept and blew her nose,
It was time to set off for the shows.

Faye James (10)
Dene House Primary School

SNAKE BITE

Off I went to the park,
On a swing I went and sat.
I thought I heard a puppy bark,
I went and gave it a pat,
Or was it a cat?
No, it was a snake,
Slash, slash, it bit like a bat.
I limped away to the lake,
Then, what I saw was not the park,
But my soul walking away.

Sean Hubery (11)
Dene House Primary School

THE FAIR

Candyfloss, lollipops,
Coca-Cola, Irn Bru.
Roller coasters zooming past,
It's my turn, at last!

Here it goes,
Up, up in the air.
Right at the top,
There's a drop.

Everyone's screaming,
Their faces are gleaming.
Now at the bottom,
The roller coaster is stopping.
Up, down, left, right,
Giving everyone such a fright!

Sophie Luckhurst (10)
Dene House Primary School

AT THE FAIR

A   is for amazing things you see,
T   is for tigers and teddies you win.

T   is for tombola and raffles to win,
H   is for shouting, *hullabaloo!*
E   is for excitement and fun.

F   is for funny clowns and tricks,
A   is for anything you want.
I   is for saying, 'I don't want to leave.'
R   is for the best ride ever.

Jamie Elves (10)
Dene House Primary School

SAD MEMORY

I remember the brown, puppy-dog eyes,
I remember the laughter and happy cries.
I was seven and he was three,
I couldn't believe he belonged to me.

The brown coat and the long fluffy tail,
He was a German shepherd - a male!
He was handsome and surely strong,
Nothing now could possibly go wrong!

One rainy, foggy, misty day,
King and I went out to play.
At five, when we came in again,
Outside it started to pour with rain.

Time to take King for a walk,
I came to the passage, I started to gawp!
He was not there, he'd vanished, he'd gone!
What did I say about nothing going wrong?

I remember the brown, puppy-dog eyes,
I remember the moans and sorrowful cries,
I remember the nights of crying and weeping,
There was no sign of ever sleeping.

Now, he's just a thought in my head,
I couldn't believe my dog was dead.
Now, I just have a picture of him,
In a pretty red picture frame.

Sarah Tough (11)
Dene House Primary School

THE FANTASTIC FAIR

The lights are all shining,
Making the sky brighten up.
You carry your Coke,
In a red paper cup.

The big, red roller coaster,
Going upside down.
The whirling waltzer,
Going round and round.

Everyone on the roller coaster,
Heaves a huge sigh,
While people in red go-karts,
Go zooming by!

Gavin McCluskey (10)
Dene House Primary School

THE PLANE JOURNEY

The noisy engine,
The large wings,
Take-off at last,
What a scary high,
A woman comes by
With a trolley,
'A refreshment, Sir?'
Spain below,
The plane lowers,
We get off,
What a relief!

Jake Unsworth (10)
Dene House Primary School

MY DREAM

I had a dream
I dived into the sea,
I wondered what I would see.
Would I see a shark
Or would I see a goldfish?
Could it be red, blue or green?
Or will there be a dark, black tunnel
That leads you into another world
Where you can eat and drink
What you want, when you want?
I would eat birthday cake and drink lemonade
Over and over again . . .
Then I would go back through the dark tunnel,
Back into the sea,
Where I see fish that are red, blue and green,
Was it all really seen
In my dream . . . ?

Abbi Newhouse (10)
Dene House Primary School

LOVE

Love is a token I hold in my heart.
Love is a festival in which to take part.
Love is a memory I hold in my head.
Love is a book, which we all have read.
Love is a song, which we all like to hear.
Love is a feeling that can cause a tear.
Love is a trance that makes people coo.
Love is the thing that I have for you!

Beth Clark (11)
Dene House Primary School

THEME PARK

In a theme park you haven't got much time,
You have to queue and climb.
The roller coaster is extremely fast,
Now we're off, the roller coaster at last.

We're on the Grand Prix ride,
Now in the House of Mirrors I must hide.
I'm in the maze, completely lost,
Never ever mind the cost!

We stumble to the way out,
We wonder what it was all about!
Mum went searching for the car,
While we lagged behind so far!

Sam Laidlaw (11)
Dene House Primary School

THE FUNFAIR

As I stand and stare
Someone wins a cuddly bear
At the fantastic, fantastic funfair.

There are roller coasters so tall,
They make me feel pretty small.
I see a fantastic stall,
I try to win a ball,
But have no luck at all.

Until my last fifty pence,
Gives me a better chance
And I win that ball!

Jack Sayers (11)
Dene House Primary School

THE DRAGON OF DOOM

Everyone is screaming,
Hair is going wild,
The tunnel is quite steaming,
Nobody to say, 'It's alright my child.'

Here we go, the triple loop!
Someone loses their hearing.
Now we are through the hoop,
Now we are here in the dragon's den.

Now the ride is stopping!
I got out, right then
And Robin was looking
At the dragon going around again.

Heather Robinson (10)
Dene House Primary School

ROLLER COASTER

Click, click, click, up we go,
All I can see are the clouds down below.
Round and round,
Down to the ground,
Swooping left, swooping right,
It was really scary up at a height.

Here we go, back down below,
Now it's going really slow.
My feet have finally touched the floor,
I'd like to go on more and more.
Click, click, click, down we go,
Zooming high, then zooming low.

Paula Mitchell (11)
Dene House Primary School

THE ROLLER COASTER

Jump on a roller coaster
Round and round we go
Whizzing round and round
Upside down we start to go!

Thinking your fears
Have all disappeared
But then, suddenly
Someone starts to scream!

Your stomach feels
As if it is tied in knots!
All you want to do
Is go and get off!

When it stops
You feel a little dizzy
Stumbling slowly, all alone
Through the crowds so busy!

Amy Moorfield (10)
Dene House Primary School

THE TEACHER'S DESK

Messy or tidy, how will it be?
The way to find out, is look and see.
Lots of rubbish, some letters and a cup,
Some files and pens, maybe a picture of a pup!
Homework sheets, papers and books,
A menu to take home, from the cooks.
Next morning everything is neat,
I think the teacher needs a treat!

Liam Knox (11)
Dene House Primary School

The Animal

One dark and gloomy night,
A little animal gave me a fright.
I don't know what it was,
I couldn't see because of the fog
Exactly what it was.

The next day, it was school,
I asked my friend - like a fool.
'Have you ever seen,
A black and white animal in the Dene?'

My friends and I went to the wood,
At the spot where I had stood.
We saw a torn, black, plastic bag
And I said to myself, 'Oh what a drag!'

James Burton (10)
Dene House Primary School

The Playground

Me and my friends love the playground,
Skipping, laughing, running around.
Hear the sound of the whistle blowing,
Now it is time for us to be going.

'Nearly home time,' the teacher says,
Hands together - time for prayers.
All of us chanting our goodnight song,
With the teacher praying along.

Jade Townley (11)
Dene House Primary School

FOOTBALL CRAZY, FOOTBALL MAD

Football crazy, football mad
Come on round and have a kick
Then go and join the lads

Running down the wing
With the ball at your feet
Trying to score and passing
To the forward - could he bend it
Like Beckham - yes!

Just as you score a goal
The opponents try hard
To pull one back
And they do
It's all square now

Nail-biting, crunching tackles
Come on lads, give us a goal
One minute of added time!
And it's a penalty - what a goal!
We win the cup!

Rhys Taylor (10)
Dene House Primary School

DOLPHINS

Dolphins can swim far away,
They are big and small,
They are grey,
Dolphins live in the sea,
I would like to watch them play
And sing their songs to me.

Tegan Stevenson (8)
Dodmire Junior School

My Baby Brother

My baby brother throws his dummy
My baby brother thinks it's funny
My baby brother makes us laugh
My baby brother loves his bath
He loves it when we come out of school
We get in the car, he thinks it's cool
He sets off laughing straightaway
'Cause he hasn't seen us all day
My baby brother loves his dinner
He's not getting any thinner
My baby brother can say 'Dad'
He won't say 'Mam', it drives her mad
That's my baby brother
I wouldn't swap him for another.

Robert Ward (9)
Dodmire Junior School

I Like Shopping

I like shopping at the shops,
Getting food for lunch,
Like sandwiches and things to crunch.
Getting new shoes that I easily lose
And posters to stick on the wall.
My mum says, 'Don't buy all those sweets.'
'But Mum, it's my week for treats,' I call.
I get a new sparkling top,
Then we go and wait at the bus stop.

Sarah Thompson (10)
Dodmire Junior School

IF ONLY

If only the skies didn't turn grey
If only people wouldn't pass away
If only I can be with you
That would make all my dreams come true

If only I could be
Whatever I wanted to be
If only you would love me
And all the people would see

Now when I make these wishes
Underneath a shooting star
I want our lives to change
But always be the people we are!

Ellie Abel (9)
Dodmire Junior School

THE WIND HOWLS, THE WIND BLOWS

The wind howls, the wind blows,
In and out of all my toes,
Out at the seaside, night and day,
Where the wind will always play,
The wind howls, the wind blows.

The wind howls, the wind blows,
Feel it rush right past your nose,
Wind causes treacherous things,
The wind sways like when birds sing,
The wind howls, the wind blows.

John Flinn (9)
Dodmire Junior School

BROOM! BROOM!

Broom! Broom!
Is the sound
Of a car going past

Broom! Broom!
Is the sound of an engine

Broom! Broom!
Is the sound of a car
Starting and finishing

Broom! Broom!
Is the sound
Of a racing car

But my car goes
Bang! Bang!

Thomas Taylor (8)
Dodmire Junior School

THE OWL

The owl is on its perch,
It hears its prey,
It dives down to catch its prey,
The mouse runs away.

He loses the mouse,
The moon is shining bright,
So he rests on a branch,
Then flies into the night.

David Lonsdale (10)
Dodmire Junior School

OWLS

Owls fly, swooping down
You often see them around the town
With eyes big and very bright
They shine in the dark night

These animals live in trees
And make different noises to the bees
Their furry feathers keep them warm
You might see them soaring when it's dawn

They can be big or very small
But that is not all
They can be white or brown
But you never see them frown.

Catherine Robinson (11)
Dodmire Junior School

STARS

Stars, they glow at night
Stars, they're really bright
Stars, they're all a pattern
Stars, they're around Saturn
Stars, they make Orion's Belt
Stars, no you have never felt
Stars, people stop to pray
Stars, they hide away for the day.

Andrew Lonsdale (9)
Dodmire Junior School

THE MONSTER

There is a monster in my cupboard
I know it without a doubt
There is a monster in my cupboard
I think I'll give my mum a shout

There is a monster in my bed
And I don't know what it has just said
There is a monster in my bed
I think I'm gonna end up dead

I'm running away just as fast as I can
Running away with the saucepan
I end the corner and scream
But hang on, it was only a dream!

Kira Bennett (10)
Dodmire Junior School

I LOVE ANIMALS

I like horses, they're my number 1,
I like others, they're my number 2,
I like bears, they're my number 3,
I like dogs, they're my number 4,
I like snakes, they're my number 5,
I like guinea pigs, they're my number 6,
I like rabbits, they're my number 7,
I like wolves, they're my number 8,
I like dolphins, they're my number 9,
I hate pigs, they're my number 10,
I like owls, my number 11.

Hannah Tinnion (10)
Dodmire Junior School

DANIEL AND ME

Daniel and me were always together
Happy days that would last forever
He was taken away
And it made me cry
He lives in a house
Up in the sky
I think of him often
And I speak his name
I look at his photo
In the wooden frame
So Daniel, if you can hear me
Listen to what I say
I care and remember you always
Every single day.

Hayley Pritchard (9)
Dodmire Junior School

IT'S NOT FAIR!

It's not fair!
I always have long hair,
I'm not allowed it cut,
Mum says I must stay put,
It's not fair!
It's not fair!
My mother's got fake hair,
She went bald at the age of *three!*
She wishes she was me!
It is fair!
I have got long hair!

Susan Sung (10)
Dodmire Junior School

A KNIGHT NOT SO STRONG AND BOLD

A knight so strong and bold,
With armour-plated gold.
He done a great deed,
Then won a steed.
At the end of the fair,
He came back with no hair.
A knight so strong and bold.

The next day he fought a man,
His name was Sir Dan.
The next day he wanted to go to war,
So he knocked down every door.
He ran back to his house,
He was as scared as a mouse.
A knight not so strong and bold.

Jo Leonard (9)
Dodmire Junior School

MY FAMILY

My family is strange
My dad's bossy and big
My sister is bald, so she has to wear a wig
My uncle is loopy, so he stands on his head
My cousin's a student, so he spends all day in bed
My aunty works for the RSPCA
She says if I don't behave they'll come for me someday
My mum loves karaoke, she thinks she's Britney Spears
But when she gets up to sing, everyone covers their ears
So as you can see, my family is strange
Did I mention my hamsters have got mange?

Kathryn Woolston (10)
Dodmire Junior School

BILLY HATES SCHOOL!

Billy hates school,
He breaks all the rules,
Stays up late on Sundays,
Sits at his desk in a gaze,
Billy hates school!

Never does his homework,
Never gets it right,
The teacher tells him off,
He gets into a fight,
Billy hates school!

Talk about the dinners,
He thinks that they're yuck,
Talk about the teachers,
He thinks they're just bad luck,
Billy hates school!

Natalie Winter (10)
Dodmire Junior School

GOD

God is here, God is there
God is always everywhere
He's down the road
Along the street
Seeing people he'll never meet
He's there when you're sleeping
And when you're awake
So you better be good
For goodness sake!

Jessica Duncan (10)
Dodmire Junior School

RELATIVES

I have an auntie Karen and a cousin called Aaran
I have an uncle Shaun and a cousin called Dawn
My auntie Diane and uncle Steve don't believe in Adam and Eve
My uncle Stu and my other auntie Di, make a smashing apple pie
My uncle Daz and my auntie Sandie, they're so fine and dandy
My younger cousins Abbey and Jodi aren't that young, they
                                        don't need a dody
My other cousins, Rachel and Nikki, well they're a bit tricky
My other cousins Mickey and Lee, well guess what? They're perfect,
                                        just like me.

Martin Hammond (10)
Dodmire Junior School

THAT TEACHER OVER THERE!

You see that teacher over there,
She does nothing but stand and stare,
She stands over there in the corner,
Like my friend, Susie Horner,
She stands over there making no sound,
Staring at the wooden ground,
In the morning when we do maths,
She stands there and looks at the graphs,
But one day she came out of there,
But she didn't stand and stare,
She came over here and gave me a hug
And from that day, I feel very snug!

Susan Glew (10)
Dodmire Junior School

SCHOOL

At school the children in Class 1 make a racket,
Charlotte, Hannah, Lesley, Nathan, Jamie,
At school the children in Class 2 open a crisp packet,
Catherine, Kira, Emily, Robert, James,
At school the children in Class 3 draw on the board,
Kimberly, Jade, Claire, Michael, John,
At school the children in Class 4 applaud,
Susan, Amy, Alice, Kieran, Joe,
At school the children in Class 5 listen smartly,
Lisa, Donna, Becky, Ashley, Josh,
At school the children in Class 6 dread Miss Heartly,
Betty, Rachael, Jacqueline, Ryan, Jacob,
At school the children in Class 7 learn lots of things,
Margaret, Katie, Laura, Mathew, Jim,
At school the children in Class 8 pretend they have wings,
Demi, Joan, Sabrina, Andrew, Jack,
At school the children in Class 9 pick their nose,
Justine, Samantha, Tracy, Peter, Joseph,
At school the children in Class 10 change their clothes,
Haley, Alison, Janet, Ayden, Jeremy,
At school the children in Class 11 get taught how to perm,
Emma, Kylie, Polly, Simon, Jerry,
But at school . . .
I learn!

Elizabeth Doubleday (10)
Dodmire Junior School

BUTTERFLIES

They flutter for weeks only,
But they are never ever lonely,
When they die, it's sad
And I feel really bad

Among the flowers they stay,
While I am there to play,
At least I can see them fly,
Before they all die.

Justine Wears (10)
Dodmire Junior School

MY PET DOG!

When I first got my loving pet,
He needed a check-up from the vet,
The vet filled a needle and gave him a prick,
To stop him becoming incredibly sick.

When the needle went in, he let out a yelp!
I stood behind not able to help,
When we got home, I gave him a hug
And wrapped him up warm in his own special rug,
He laid in his bed and fell fast asleep,
He stayed there all night, not a sound, not a peep.

Charlie, my dog, is now one year old,
A beautiful dog, so I've been told,
I play with my dog when I get home from school,
I think he's the best, he's funny and cool,
He likes to play football when we go to the park,
He sleeps on my bed because he's afraid of the dark!

Charlie, my dog, is my most trusted friend,
Although he can drive me round the *bend!*
I will love him forever, that is a bet,
Because Charlie to me, is the best ever *pet!*

Samantha McPhee (8)
Dodmire Junior School

WHY ARE YOU LATE FOR SCHOOL?

I didn't get up
Because I slept in
And I slept in
Because I was tired
And I was tired
Because I went to bed late
And I went to bed late
Because I was writing a story
And I was writing a story
Because Miss asked me to
And Miss asked me to
Because I didn't do one in class
And I didn't do one in class
Because I wasn't listening
And I wasn't listening
Because I was looking out the window
And I was looking out the window
Because I saw a fly
I am late Sir
Because I saw a fly!

Charlotte Wiper (10)
Dodmire Junior School

MY BEST FRIEND

My best friend does everything for me
My best friend is always there
My best friend helps me when I'm down
My best friend gets rid of my frown.

Shannon Mooney (8)
Dodmire Junior School

SUMMER

Summer weaves across the land
Follow her and take her hand
She will lead you glorious places
See lots of scenes and lots of faces
The sun shines down with golden rays
She walks the land for all her days
Her delicate hands touch simmered soil
And flowers sprout and ivy toil
Her eyes forever weep to the ground
Where grass will spread for far around
Her golden hair makes golden corn
Her blood-red lips make rose and thorn
And where her feet may tread
Watch as the life will spread
So when summer weaves across the land
Follow her and take her hand.

Rebecca Hindmarch (11)
Dodmire Junior School

DARK AT NIGHT

What does the dark do at night?
When you have a fright
On the way through the meadow
The flowers are there and the sun is bare
So you're with your jolly good fellow
The trees are telling you tonight
You will have a fright
Swaying and lulling all the night
So what does the dark do at night?

Amy Bearpark (9)
Dodmire Junior School

SPACE ALIENS

Once I saw a space alien, coming from above,
More louder than a lion, more silent than a dove,
This creature was very strange, he had never heard of love,
But I still liked him, so I took him back above.

Nicholas Wiper (8)
Dodmire Junior School

THE BEST SEASIDE EVER

The best seaside is the one under the hot sun
Yes, the one with the golden sand
Yes, to be there would be grand
That's the best seaside ever
Understand!

Paige Mooney (10)
Dodmire Junior School

APPLES AND ORANGES

Apples and oranges
Are growing on the trees
All good fruit just for me
I will pick one and then another
And leave the rest for my big brother.

Rebecca Wilson (10)
Durham Gilesgate Primary School

OUR TEACHERS

The school where we go is very neat.
A lot of our teachers are really quite upbeat.
There's Mr Turner who is the head,
Who is bright and bushy when he gets out of bed.
Yeah.
Then there's Mr Bryson who teaches us well,
All of his classes are really swell.
*More like H***!*
There's Mrs Russell, the drama queen,
She's very good at making a scene.
Sit down and behave.
There's Mrs March, the calendar lass,
Who is very nice to all our class.
As if!
Then there's Mr Weetman, the cereal guy,
You will laugh so much, you will want to cry.
More like cry!
There's Mrs Toole, who helps run the school,
Now and again she will bend a rule.
But when?
There's Mrs Elliot who can play a good tune,
When you sing well, she is over the moon.
With a rocket!
There's Mrs Bell, I've had as well,
A really good story she knows how to tell.
Yawn.
But overall they are all very nice,
As the rhyme goes, they are like sugar and spice.

Stephen Mickle (10)
Durham Gilesgate Primary School

THE 4 SEASONS

The summer brings great joy,
To me, such a little boy.
I like to run, jump and play,
That makes my day.
The late night,
The morning so bright.
The morning's scorching hot sun,
Goes down well with my drink and bun.
Barbeques, food and drinks,
All we need now is a cool ice rink.

Autumn is here,
The air is clear.
The leaves have fallen
And the wind is calling.
I like to kick the leaves up high,
So it looks like they are falling from the sky.
The fire is lit,
The fireworks are fit.
Guy Fawkes is sad,
Wasn't he bad?

Lying on the ground is the snow,
The sledges don't half go.
Snow is falling,
Snowball fights all around,
I am calling.
Snowmen are all over the ground,
Stockings are really full.
I open my presents with a pull,
Melted as the snow,
Oh, I didn't want it to go.

Birds are flying,
New lambs are crying.
Flowers are blossoming nice,
Run away do the little mice.
Bees buzz from here to there,
Stinging people without a care.
I like to run, jump and play,
As I enjoy my day.
The summer is nearly here again,
So I think I'll take a walk down the lane.

Dean Cowan (10)
Durham Gilesgate Primary School

ON WINTER DAYS

On winter days when everything is white,
It's sometimes not a very good sight.
On winter days when snow is falling from the sky,
Twizzling, twirling from so high.
On winter days the snow is calm,
It cannot do you any harm.
On winter days when the path is ice,
You don't see many rats or mice.
On winter days when children play . . .
In the snow they play all day.
On winter days when the grass is white,
It sometimes stays like that all through the night.
On winter days you get frostbites,
Some people play with their kites.
On winter days it's hailstoning,
It looks a lot like it is snowing.
On winter days it's very fun,
Winter days for everyone.

Jordan Nicholson (9)
Durham Gilesgate Primary School

The Months Of The Year

February, March, April, May
Is a time to come out to play.
The lambs are born, flowers grow,
Even the grass needs a mow.

June, July, August
Is a time to have some fun.
Let's go to the beach and play in the sun.
Building sandcastles all day long,
Off home now singing a merry old song.

September, October,
Time to wrap up warm.
The nights are getting colder,
Wrap up tight in your bed.

November, December,
Is a time for celebration,
For Jesus was born this very night.
So put your arms around someone
And hold them tight.
Jesus loves everyone, every day and night.

Amy Foster (9)
Durham Gilesgate Primary School

Welcome To The Haunted House

Step in through the rusty gates
Be as quiet as a mouse
We're going to sneak and take a peak
Inside the haunted house!

Ghosts are hooting in the hallway
Ghastly ghouls lurk on the stairs
Imps and sprites have pillow fights
To catch you unawares!

Upstairs in the dusty bedrooms
Skeletons are getting dressed
Vampires brush their hair and teeth
All spooks must look their best!

So while the party's in full swing
Be quiet as a mouse
Tiptoe out while you still can
Escape the haunted house!

Rachael Staff (10)
Durham Gilesgate Primary School

CHRISTMAS

Christmas is a happy time,
When the bells in Heaven chime,
All the little girls and boys,
Are happy with their Christmas toys.

All the mums and dads go to ski,
Up the slopes and around the tree,
Up, down, up, down and around they go,
Having fun in the silky snow.

At home again having fun,
All the hard work has been done,
Everyone sitting by the Christmas tree,
Getting ready for a yummy tea.

In bed everyone snuggles down,
Trying to hear the sounds of the busy town,
But no one can hear, not a peep,
Everyone must be fast asleep.

Stephanie Foster (10)
Durham Gilesgate Primary School

OUR GARDEN

Digging in the garden,
Pulling up the weeds,
Raking all the stones away,
Sowing little seeds.

Growing flowers for Mother,
Parsley for the cook,
Finding how to treat them,
In the garden book.

Bringing friends to each
Pretty garden bed,
Surely this is pleasant work
For Rose and Ned.

Rebecca Mason (9)
Durham Gilesgate Primary School

ON THE SEASIDE

Mermaid, mermaid, under the sea,
Would you please come and fetch me?
Swimming with the fishes is something I'd like to do,
But I'd like to be a bird too.
Why do seagulls sing in the sky?
The wind is blowing high, so high.
I sit here in the sand, dreaming of what I'd like to be,
High in the sky or down in the sea.

Jade Sharp (9)
Durham Gilesgate Primary School

MY DAY

I go to school each day
I'm happy at my work
I love to read and write
And do my homework every night

After we've had our lunch
We go outside to play
I play with all my friends
Jane and Joan and Kay

When I go home from school
I get changed to go to Guides
We learn first aid and songs
With Brown Owl at our side.

Reanne Finnigan (11)
Durham Gilesgate Primary School

AT THE BOTTOM OF MY GARDEN

The roses in my garden
Grow by my garden shed
Sheltered from the wind you see
And they grow in a nice soft bed

The blossom of my roses
Is very sweet indeed
At the bottom of my garden
Come the honeybees.

Cameron Dodd (9)
Durham Gilesgate Primary School

MY PETS

I had a dog whose name was Bobby,
He liked running, it was his favourite hobby.
I have a rabbit whose name is Gizmo,
He likes to eat carrots, they're his favourite food.
Sometimes he gets in a really bad mood.
I had a frog whose name was Filbert,
When he was ill, my mam called him Illbert.
I have a bird whose name is Strawberry,
She feels really merry.
I have a fish whose name is Goldy,
Sometimes her fish tank gets smelly and mouldy.
I had another fish whose name was Spot,
He was really tiny, he was like a dot.
I had yet another fish whose name was Billy,
He was a good fish, he was really silly.

Stacey Archer (10)
Easington Colliery Primary School

THE THING UNDER MY BED

The thing under my bed is frightful and scary
The thing under my bed is awfully hairy
The thing under my bed has big booming eyes
The thing under my bed made me jump in surprise!

The thing under my bed makes me want my flashlight
The thing under my bed makes me scream in the night
The thing under my bed makes me have nightmares
The thing under my bed gives me the chills and the scares.

Sarah Marine (10)
Easington Colliery Primary School

MUNGLE IN THE JUNGLE

Mungle in the jungle, mungle in the jungle
What a fuss, mungle in the jungle

Monkeys screaming and still showing off
Jaguars roaring and the rain is pouring
Centipedes crawling and they are all bawling
Panthers are relaxing and they are clawing

Mungle in the jungle, mungle in the jungle
What a commotion, mungle in the jungle

Mungle, tungle in the jungle!
What a *fuss!*
Mungle in the *jungle!*

Jonathan Turnbull (11)
Easington Colliery Primary School

RAINBOWS

Red is for roses,
Which smell quite sweet,
Orange is an orange,
Which is better than meat,
Yellow is for cheese,
'That's tasty,' say mice,
Green is for grass,
That's soft and nice,
Blue is for the sea,
That's cold and deep,
Violet is for the flower,
That I devour.

Gemma Middleton (11)
Easington Colliery Primary School

FOOTBALL

Football is the best game ever
It's a great game with a ball
I'd want to play it whatever the weather
It's the best game of them all

I like Allesandro Del Piero
He is really quite a hero
I hate Sunderland
They really should be Blunderland

Ronaldo is the best
He could beat the rest
I like Henry
He is not a donkey

Shearer scores goals
He does not hit the post
Kevin Phillips can't score
He can't get a goal

Seaman is so old
He should not be in goal
Sunderland are number 20
They cannot win, they need plenty.

Nathan Forster (11)
Easington Colliery Primary School

WOLF SONG

Deep in the woods there lives a wolf
Who has a litter of cubs
They like to cuddle and huddle up tight
But will they survive the winter's night?

In the morning they are very frisky
But by the river, it's very risky
By their mum they are safe and sound
But you never know, they might be found.

Rachael Huitson (11)
Easington Colliery Primary School

THE WEATHER

Whatever the weather
It's sure to show
I'm almost certain
It's likely to glow

Sometimes it's cool
Sometimes it's sunny
Sometimes it's rainy
But I think it's funny

The snow is the coldest
It's one of the best
I don't like the rain
It's not like the rest

The weather is cool
Whatever it's like
One thing's for sure
I know you'll like

Whatever the weather
It's sure to show
I'm almost certain
It's likely to glow.

Sarah Naisbett (11)
Easington Colliery Primary School

LILLIAN LUSAVICH

Lillian Lusavich is a lovely girl
She has a big, wide smile
And teeth like pearls

Lillian Lusavich has two best friends
Ned and Sarah
Their friendship will never end

Lillian Lusavich has a dog named Sprout
He has leaping, long legs
And a really long snout

Lillian Lusavich has a mum and dad
They take her to theme parks
Such as Disney Land

Lillian Lusavich is a lovely girl
She has a big, wide smile
And teeth like pearls.

Jennifer Adamson (10)
Easington Colliery Primary School

SPLASHING!

Splashing in the water all day long,
Making everyone laugh.
Doing tricks to show everyone
And some people think it is daft.

One, two, three, splashing all day,
It's real, really happy in May.
One, two, three, splashing all day,
It's real, real happy in May.

Time to go, she is alone,
Very unhappy and very cold.
Time to have fun,
Very happy and very hot.

One, two, three, splashing all day,
It's real, real happy in May.
One, two, three, splashing all day,
It's real, real happy in May.

Sarah Heppell (10)
Easington Colliery Primary School

SNOW DAY

I go outside and what do I see?
Twelve inches of snow covering me!
I grab my gloves and roll a ball,
To my amazement there's more snowfall.

'I'll build the best snowman in the land,
Better than building a castle of sand.'
I build a head and a body and when I'm done,
My clothes are soggy.

I use a carrot for the nose
And for the eyes, a piece of coal,
Very soon it's half-past three,
I sit and rest under a tree.

Shortly, night begins to fall,
Guided by a frosted moon,
I go inside,
It's bedtime soon.

Craig Williamson (11)
Easington Colliery Primary School

MY AMBITIONS

I've decided, I've decided,
What my ambition is to be,
I would love to be famous,
So this is just right for me.

I'd like to be a news reporter
Or even a midwife.
My mum says I'm a good singer,
But I think she needs to think twice.

I'd love my family to be proud of me
And help me to achieve a fascinating career,
But most of all I'd like to be myself
And put my ideas to a stop,
Till my mind is crystal clear.

Anna Constance Hewitson (11)
Easington Colliery Primary School

MY HAMSTER

My hamster has a tiny nose
My hamster has sharp little toes

My hamster loves to play in its ball
My hamster does the monkey bars on the cage wall

My hamster is kind and gentle
My hamster runs around like mental

I've bought my hamster lots of toys
My hamster makes a lot of noise.

Laura Elwell (11)
Easington Colliery Primary School

THE POLAR BEAR

Ice in their eyes
Frost in their paws
The poor, cold, shivering
Polar bear

No hope in store
Just sadness galore
The weak, tired
Polar bear

Their tired eyes
Their babies weak
Sadness, sadness
No luck or love
The cold, hungry, tearful
Polar bear.

Alexandra Chapman (10)
Easington Colliery Primary School

TWO DOGS

L   is for my puppy, Lucy, who loves to bark and play around
U   is for underestimating the energy my puppy has inside
C   is for how cute she is when she is lying on the ground
Y   is for how young she is when running along the tide

And

T   is for my big dog, Tess, who lies without a sound
E   is for how energetic she acts when she is old
S   is for how sweet she is when she is lying on the ground
S   is for how suddenly she loves to make me proud.

Terri-Anne Cooper (11)
Easington Colliery Primary School

ANIMALS GALORE

Most are cute, some are vicious
Lions think raw meat is delicious

Some are black, some are white
Some come out during the night

Animals are kept as pets
The bad thing is, you have to take them to the vet's

You go to the zoo to see them all
If you want to see some more, don't go to the mall

I love animals better than all the rest
But my hamster, Bundle, has to be the best.

Sarah Emerson (10)
Easington Colliery Primary School

FUDGE, MY DOG

Fudge is the best
He loves to play
Along with the rest
And jump along in the hay

He runs after a stick
And makes himself sick
We take him for a walk
Straight to the park

When he gets home
He goes for a roam
Tears up my poem
But he's still the best!

Alex Birbeck (10)
Easington Colliery Primary School

MY FAVOURITE DOG

S   is for Sheba, that is her name
H   is for the happiness she gives us every day
E   is for the energy that she has
B   is for the barking that she does all the time
A   is for the anger, when she sees Holly

Sheba is the best
When she is at rest

She jumps all day
But she never ever strays

She barks all the time
And jumps up at the washing line.

Gemma Black (10)
Easington Colliery Primary School

PETS

My rabbit lives inside its hutch
And likes to hop and run.
She loves to eat the cabbage leaves
And play in the blazing sun.

My tortoise lives in a large glass tank,
His shell is as hard as a nail!
When he is happy, he climbs onto his log
And wiggles his stumpy tail!

My goldfish lives in the aquarium
And they dart about all day,
They eat lots and lots of goldfish food
And their birthday is in May.

Rachel Handy (11)
Easington Colliery Primary School

TOON ARMY!

Alan Shearer is the best,
He can bounce the ball off his chest,
He kicks a ball all day long,
Then he starts to sing a song.

Lua Lua can spar,
But he can only go so far,
He plays football and wears a vest,
Then he has to have a rest.

Bobby Robson is the king
And so he wears a big fat ring.

Bellamy comes from Wales
And he goes to all of the top sales,
Bellamy kicks the ball so high,
It goes flying into the sky.

Andy O'Brien has a big nose
And when he scores, he likes to pose.

Toon Army are the best
And they will never rest!

Carly Moore (10)
Easington Colliery Primary School

ALIENS

Aliens, aliens, where do you come from?
We come from a land called Crom.

We live on a planet named Mars,
We never see cars.

We talk very strange,
We can see long range.

We are very green and slimy,
We are not very keen on baked beans.

We don't know what to do,
But we could go to a do.

We went on a spaceship,
We ate an apple with a pip.

Ashleigh Westmoreland (10)
Easington Colliery Primary School

NEWCASTLE TEAM

Alan Shearer is the best
He kicks the ball in the net
Even though he is depressed
Sometimes he has a bet

Shay Given dives for the ball
Even though he always falls
He thought he was going to die
So he always cries

Loo ar Lud is so springy
He could do backflips for the world
In 5 minutes later he'll be in a dinghy
Then when he stopped, he twirled

Bobby Robson is so old
He makes a fortune off his gold
Then he bribed the referee
To win the game, to win for me.

Faye Johnson (10)
Easington Colliery Primary School

THE MOON

I'm grey and bright
In the night I shine light
I am way up high
I see people in their ties
Every night I fly
Then I say bye

People look at me in the eye
I like smelling pie
I hate to see people die
I love to lie
I am the good guy

From way up in the sky
Just why
I never cry
I can be shy
So now goodbye.

Martyn Robinson (11)
Easington Colliery Primary School

FOOTBALL CRAZY, WORLD CUP MAD

Football crazy, World Cup mad,
England Vs Brazil, England go mad,
Brazil get hammered to one side,
England get pushed back to the other,
Owen blacks Ronaldo's eye,
Beckham blacks the other,
Hooray for England,
England are the class,
England beat Brazil in the 1st class.

Mykal Hutton (10)
Easington Colliery Primary School

TELEVISION

We need it!
We want it!
Television!
Television is the thing we must have,
Television rules,
They even have it in schools,
When we get bored, we can turn it on,
Match Of The Day is on BBC1,
When we watch television you want to chill,
But when the footie comes on, it's more like a thrill,
We all love television,
Sometimes I like to sit and watch a film,
When you watch a drama,
You will get calmer,
We need it!
We want it!
Television!

Stuart Muir (11)
Easington Colliery Primary School

MY DOG

S   asha is a greyhound
A   t six o'clock in the morning, she jumps onto my bed
S   he loves to play with my frisbee
H   appy she is when she gets dizzy
A   ll the time she licks my head

She is the best dog in the world
I love my dog!

Louise Parkin (11)
Easington Colliery Primary School

SHOPPING

Every Monday
Somehow, some way
We always end up going

Buying food
Shoppers being rude
Trolleys dashing
Crashing and bashing
Faster, faster
But remember the pasta

Every Sunday
Somehow, some way
We always run out of food.

Connor Robson (11)
Easington Colliery Primary School

QUINNS AND PHILLIPS

Niall Quinns' disco pants are the best
They come from his ass to his chest

They are better than Alan Shearer's
Niall Quinns' disco pants are the best

Super, super, super Kev
Super, super, super Kev
Super, super, super Kev
Super Kevin Phillips

Oh Tommy, Tommy
Oh Tommy, Tommy
Oh Tommy, Tommy Sorenson.

David Robinson (11)
Easington Colliery Primary School

MY FRIENDS

My friends are very odd,
One loves art, the other one hates it
And when it comes to do PE teams,
I can hardly choose,
But one thing's for sure,
When it comes to sleepovers,
All of us make it a night to remember.

We all hang out at school,
We all try to talk at weekends.

We may not live near each other,
But in the six-week holiday, all of us have fun.

You think you can only have one best friend,
But you can't, all of your close friends can be best friends
Because I have three best friends!

Danielle Kenney (11)
Easington Colliery Primary School

SPIDER TRICKS

Jumping spiders are great to see
They are not my favourite thing
Their webs are like diamond rings
The spider's fangs are like sharp daggers
The spider's poison is like citric acid
It will burn a hole in your stomach
The spider's legs are like very long broomsticks
The way they walk is creepy
So be very careful
They will pounce on you!

Anna Chapman (10)
Easington Colliery Primary School

RAT

I know a rat who lives in an alley
But sometimes he goes doolally

He goes in the butcher's shop and nearly gets his tail chopped off
On my way home he has a chase off

He loses the cat and he eats his meat
He sits next to the fire and it gives off heat

He burnt his tail once and it hurt
He was eating lots of meat and I burped

He nearly got eaten once and he had a heart attack
He eats his food and it all cracks

He goes to sleep
In a big heap

He goes to his friend's house and the next morning
He is yawning

I know a rat who lives in an alley
But sometimes he goes doolally.

Andrew Cook (10)
Easington Colliery Primary School

GOD

God made whisky,
God made Pepsi,
God made you so mint and sexy,
God made rivers,
God made lakes,
God made us but we all make mistakes.

Amy Louise Bradley (11)
Easington Colliery Primary School

SPLASHING DOLPHIN

Splashing through the water is Bellos
All fish think that he is chaos

Shouting from the sand is a boy
And all the sailors say is 'Ahoy'

Singing is Bellos in the middle of the night
And some of his friends are a bit of a fright

Fishermen try to catch him but they just get splashed
And they all get bashed

Disturbing all the children in bed
But if he doesn't, he gets a bad head

Jumping and swimming with all his friends
And sometimes when he jumps he sees some hens.

Lauren Fenwick (10)
Easington Colliery Primary School

CROCODILE

The jaws that bite,
The claws that catch,
The feet that kick.

Prepare now before you get a fright,
It's worse than a pirate that has an eyepatch,
Don't shoot him or you'll go in the nick,
He has more rage in water than on land,
When he's caged, he'll run wild on you,
That's the personality of the *crocodile*.

Christopher Parker (10)
Easington Colliery Primary School

BLUE ROSE

Blue petals all day long,
Everyone sings the sweetest song.

Bushy, spiky, tall and green,
Roses are never ever so mean.

Swishing and swirling, it likes to play,
The best month is the first of May.

It feels happy, sometimes sad,
It never felt a little mad.

It really, really loves the rain,
I don't think it's got any pain.

It lives in the garden beside the tree
And it really doesn't bother me.

It sits by the three trees beside the window,
In rain, shine or snow.

Blue petals all day long,
Everyone sings the sweetest song.

Chelsea Price (11)
Easington Colliery Primary School

ALIEN HORROR

As his UFO flies
He stands there with his red eyes
He is so green
He even looks mean

His favourite food is meat
But he hates the heat
He may look scary
But he can't be hairy

Sometimes he's nasty
He likes his pasties
He's really kind
But no one minds

He likes to fly
In the black sky
As he flies
He looks out and sees a red planet.

Amy Wilson (10)
Easington Colliery Primary School

CRAZY ALIEN

There is a crazy thing up in the sky
I think it might be trying to fly

It's going round and round, up and down
It might be a clown

I think it's going up to space
It might have a funny face

It has got a very slow voice
I don't think it's got a choice

What if it lives on the moon?
He might have a song that goes in tune

What if it is a weird-shaped alien
And it has a pet chameleon?

It might be a girl
And have lots of curls.

Beccy Bradley (11)
Easington Colliery Primary School

DOG

His name is Spotty
Because he is dotty

He looks fake
I think he is easy to make

He always scatters
But it doesn't matter

Spotty is always clowning around
But one day he went bound

He is a boy
He likes his toy

He likes to play
Every day

Spotty is fair
But he is rare

He can hear
And he has a fear.

Rebecca Turnbull (10)
Easington Colliery Primary School

THE UFO

Shooting through the universe
In his UFO
Flying past the galaxy
But he's going nowhere

Blasting past the Earth
Not knowing what it's worth
Floating past Mars
And dreaming about cars

Speeding through Jupiter
At top speed
Cruising past Saturn
He's almost home

Shooting through the universe
In his UFO
Flying past the galaxy
And now he's home.

David Green (10)
Easington Colliery Primary School

THE SUN

I'm big and bright
In the night,
I produce light
I'm shiny brown
Like a king's golden crown
I see many faces
Passing by many places
Some people sunbathe
Some people find a cave
I like my colour gold
Every day I get old
Sometimes I go red
When people are in bed
When I'm hot, I rule
Some people think I'm cool
I watch people go to school
But they wish they were in a pool.

Martyn Corrigan (10)
Easington Colliery Primary School

TROUBLE

T   rouble is bad and you make people feel sad
R   age is when you're mad and you get told off from your dad
O   is an offence, when you break somebody's fence
U   is unseemly behaviour and you'll definitely not be in favour
B   is when you bicker and get on somebody's wick
L   is when you're late, late with your homework
E   is for an eventful day, you put blue dye in the pool
    All this spells *trouble.*

Jonathon Lewins (11)
Easington Colliery Primary School

HATE!

Hate is like an ocean of deep doomed anger
Slithering up to my immortal soul
Scaring and smothering me so I can hardly breathe

Hate is a horrifying huddle of bloodstained demons
Waiting to come and explode my red, dripping blood; making me boil

Hate is a big blanket of bloodthirsty, dangerous devils
Following me everywhere I go

Hate is a computer virus of deadly ghosts
Solidifying my face into a horrible mask of terror

Hate is like a cruel kidnapper
Coming to abduct me and take me to his lair

Making my blood run cold
Making me his *victim!*

Zoe Stones (9)
Ludworth Primary School

NIGHT

Night is like an abandoned factory
Staring at the dark houses

Night is a place where there isn't any light

Night is like an abandoned house
Watching people walk along the street coming home from work

Night is like a damp warehouse
Sitting on the north coast waiting for someone to come in

Night is like a foggy sea
Scaring me as I lie in my cosy bed.

Helen Atkinson (10)
Ludworth Primary School

NIGHT

Night is like a black spider
Lurking around the garden

Night is like a dark, mysterious figure
Searching to see what he can steal

Night is like a small gnome
Bobbing up and down, blocking the light

Night is like a mysterious robber
Running over the long fields.

Scott Carter (9)
Ludworth Primary School

THE NIGHT FRIGHT

Night is a coffin full of horrors
Watching you as it slithers like a python
With sharp teeth covered in poison

Night is like a giant monster
Coming closer and closer to give you a fright
By wrapping you in a thorny tomb

Night is like a black hole growing bigger
And more powerful, pulling you in

Night is like a gloomy, haunted graveyard.

Craig Whittle (10)
Ludworth Primary School

DARK

Dark is like a big, tall shadow
Looking at the little gnome

Dark is like a tall robber
Watching the spider creep up the garden path

Dark is like a gnome
Flashing in the dead of the night

Dark is like the robber
Sneaking around the garden.

Rachel Nadine Stabler (9)
Ludworth Primary School

SPACE

Space is like a dark black cupboard
Covering me in bright, glittering stars
And a silent rocket with burning flames shooting around me

Space is like a big colourful box
Crowding me with lots of shapes
And an astronaut buzzing around me

Space is like a dark, dark house
Blanketing me with a double-coated star blanket
And a spaceship cushion

Space is like the dusty Earth
Coming towards me in my little spaceship.

Jonathan Kell (9)
Ludworth Primary School

A WARRIOR

A warrior is like a big, green army tank
Crushing people's bones into dust as it fires its bullets

A warrior is like a huge, powerful aeroplane
Bombing anything that gets in its way

A warrior is like a sharp, terrifying sword
Cutting people's heads off as it swoops

A warrior is like a big, frightening gun
Shooting people through their thumping hearts.

Matt Keeble (9)
Ludworth Primary School

LIGHTNING

Lightning is like a black electric chair
Striking you with a whip of electricity
That scares you, terrifies you, kills you

Lightning is like an illuminated knife
Spying on you and waiting to strike your every move
You cannot hide; you cannot run, so watch out, beware!

Lightning is like a yellow laser beam
Hitting you through the forest; through the houses' roofs

Lightning is like an overgrown pylon
Falling on you, trying to catch you, trying to get you.

Jonathan Sutherland (9)
Ludworth Primary School

WINTER

Winter is like a thousand pieces of white paper
Scattering all around me, slowly making me feel like a snowman

Winter is like a huge silky white box
Shrinking while the sun gets higher and higher

Winter is like an ice-cold freezer
Melting its way down to summer

Winter is like a hard white boulder
Blazing down from the tops of the sky to the bottom of the ground.

Kieryn Heseltine (10)
Ludworth Primary School

SUNLIGHT

Sunlight is like colourful candy cones
Sparkling on the grass

Sunlight is like a beautiful butterfly
Dancing through the trees

Sunlight is like the morning
Peering through the window

Sunlight is like a yellow flash
Covering my garden gnome.

Hannah Critchlow (8)
Ludworth Primary School

DARK

Dark is like a black rat
Watching every shadow

Dark is like a gnome
Sitting on the garden path

Dark is like a robber
Crawling towards the gnome

Dark is like a mysterious shadow
Running away from the house.

Kate Critchlow (8)
Ludworth Primary School

BRIGHT

Bright is like a morning sun
Peeping over the trees

Bright is like the colourful flowers
Waving at me as I look out the window

Bright is like a huge flashing sun
Shining on my gnome

Bright is like the sparkly rain
Crying because my gnome has gone

Bright is like a yellow blanket
Covering my garden

Bright is no more.

Stevie-Leigh Hall (8)
Ludworth Primary School

KEEP OUR PLANET TIDY

Our planet will become a tip if we don't look after it
Use bins and recycling tins, that's how to keep our planet tidy
Don't throw rubbish in the sea, this is up to you and me
Take this script, put it in your mind
Then you will never leave a piece of scrap behind

Please keep our planet tidy!

Toni Edwards (11)
Ludworth Primary School

Morning

Morning is like a red flame
Flowing through the grass

Morning is like a tiny little bird
Flying through the bright blue sky

Morning is like a big red sun
Lurking around the house

Morning is like a big tall man
Watching out of his window

Morning is like the foggy clouds
Covering my garden gnome.

Daniel Lee (8)
Ludworth Primary School

Sunshine

Sunshine is like a fire
Warming my back as I sit in the garden

Sunshine is like my pink and red flowers
Peeping over the flowerpots

Sunshine is like a man
Staring at his colourful garden, looking for my gnome

Sunshine is like the sunlight
Falling, I no longer can see my gnome fishing.

Andrew Whittle (8)
Ludworth Primary School

CREATURE OF THE NIGHT

When the owl is sitting on the gatepost waiting for prey
It hoots like the howling wind

When the owl spots its prey
And swoops down on it with wings outspread
It is a waterfall tumbling over a jagged cliff

When the owl glides along
It is a jet speeding to the base

When the owl's big round eyes shine
They're like the moon on a calm night

When the owl's white and grey feathers twinkle in the moonlight
They are snowflakes falling from the sky.

Benjamin Brown (11)
Ouston Junior School

CREATURE OF THE NIGHT

When the owl swoops down to catch its prey
It is a waterfall crashing to the surface

When the owl sits on the gatepost so still
It is like a statue frozen in one place

Its pale white face is like a garden of snow

When the owl grabs its prey
It is the frost gripping all living things

When the owl glides through the air
It is the wind freely flying through the night sky.

Jack Aiston (10)
Ouston Junior School

THE WIND

I rummage across the garden like a roaring lion,
Swiftly bending the flowers as I gently pluck the petals off,
Stripping the branches as bare as night.
I lift the sea noisily
And drop it fiercely,
I dash past the rooftops and dodge the rain,
I take the scent of sweet lavender
And spread it across the fields as quick as a flash.
I run for miles like a cheetah catching its prey
Or just swiftly move the washing line in the opposite direction.
I turn the umbrellas inside out quickly,
As I moan and groan,
Along the wet pathway.

Lindsey Wharton (11)
Ouston Junior School

THE WIND

It is a murderer,
Devouring homes and robbing people of their lives,
Slashing past your face in pleasure,
Ranting and raving in your ears,
Prancing and dancing with the clothes on the washing line,
Clashing and cursing as it moves through the air,
Bending and breaking the branches of a tree,
Stealing through a garden and rippling the waters of a pond;
Causing the people of Earth to quiver and shiver,
Roaring and soaring up into the sky,
Then settling down for the night.

Abigail Forster (10)
Ouston Junior School

CREATURE OF THE NIGHT

When a vampire bat drinks blood
It is a loveless werewolf.
Bats are as blind as a silly old man.
When a bat moves between the trees
It is the silent death.
When a bat is in danger
It makes high-pitched squeaks
Like an upset mouse.
Bats are as grey as a mad devil.
When a bat is frightened
It attacks you as if it is a grizzly bear.
When a bat is in the light
It flaps its wings like a leaping tiger.
A bat hovers in the air
Like a peewee eating a flower.
The bat soars through the air
Like a fox chasing a rabbit.
When a bat is asleep
It is a dark black shadow.

Sally Ann Rawlinson (11)
Ouston Junior School

GREEN

Green is grass, cold and wet.
Green is leaves floating past.
Green is a T-rex stamping its feet.
Green is a lizard eating a fly.
Green is a colour of a beautiful rainbow.
Green is a spike of a very big cactus.

Samuel Johnson (9)
Ouston Junior School

THE WIND

I am a fierce greyhound,
I can barge through the gate
And creep into the garden,
I can rustle through the bushes
And I can ripple through the water in the pond as quick as a missile,
Or blow flames out in my pathway.
I can scream and shout as loud as a hurt baby after falling down.
I moan and groan like an injured warrior dying on a battlefield
And carry the scent of a beautiful red rose.
I can change the weather easily
And blow the cobwebs away
Or blow in different directions
And knock the heads off the flowers in the flower beds.
I can rip branches off trees
Or move swiftly, then stop
And sleep like a sleepy baby.

Philip Harland (11)
Ouston Junior School

ORANGE

Orange, the colour of freshly grown carrots,
Just pulled out of the ground.
Orange is the colour of a warm, glowing fire
And the smell of fresh, cool orange juice.
Orange peel is the feel of a snake's rough, scaly skin.
Orange, orange, wonderful orange,
The sound of crunching autumn leaves.
The colour of a glowing sunrise in the mottled sky.
Orange is the colour of a warm hat and gloves to match.

Rachael Yeadon (9)
Ouston Junior School

THE WIND

I am an eagle,
Perching on a mountain in silence, asleep,
Then gradually creeping into the air,
Getting faster and stronger than ever before,
Eventually I soar through the sky.
I brush the grass and claw at hair,
Pulling and tugging in rage.
As I near lakes I stroke the water with my fingers,
Rippling it as I go,
Devouring leaves in a beastly manner.
Calling, roaring, howling frantically,
Yet never waking the flowers or creatures.
As I near the mountains I calm down,
Eventually sleeping.

Lauren Patterson (11)
Ouston Junior School

THE COLOUR OF BLUE

Blue is the colour of the sky above
And the shivering sea at the seaside.
Blue is the colour of sadness,
It's the only crayon in the box
That makes me stop and think
Of the sea slipping through my fingers.
Blue is also the colour of water,
Not just in the sea but
Clean water makes us healthy every day.
Even though it's the colour of sadness,
I don't know what we'd do without it!

Katie Rebecca Hampson (9)
Ouston Junior School

MY GRANDMA'S GREAT BUT SHE'S LOST SOME WEIGHT!

As Grandma lay in her bed,
A pillow rests beneath her head.
Machines are talking,
While Grandad's walking,
'How are you?' the doctor said.

Theatre over, doing well,
Patients pushing on the bell.
Nurses come and bustle by,
Making sure no one dies.

Lights are flashing, wires drip,
Grandma takes her water sips.
Two by two the relatives troop,
Not allowed as a large group.

I wrote this poem especially for you,
To cheer you up when you are blue.
The message is clear from us to you,
Heaven can wait, cos we love you.

Chelsey Brittany Parker (10)
Ouston Junior School

BLUE

Blue is a colour for sadness,
Blue is the colour of the sky above us,
Blue is the colour of the sea,
Blue is the colour of tap water in your house,
Blue is the colour of ice in the freezing cold winter,
Blue is in all different things,
So look for the colour blue.

Rachel Laidler (9)
Ouston Junior School

ORANGE

Orange is fire, too hot to touch,
Orange is the warmth of a fire, blazing bright,
Orange is an orange and also the mango,
Orange is a tiger with a fierce attack,
Orange is a fox, sly and sharp,
Orange is fire, too hot to touch.

Jack Thirlwell (9)
Ouston Junior School

A SPIDER'S LEGS

The first leg is like an extra large matchmaker,
The second leg is like the tall, skinny neck of a giraffe,
The third leg is like an old, wobbly, tall lamp post,
The fourth leg is like an extra large blade of grass,
The fifth leg is like a straw for a giant,
The sixth leg is like a long washing line dangling in the air,
The seventh leg is like an extra long stick of liquorice,
The eighth leg is like five men on top of each other.

Anna Drake (8)
Ouston Junior School

PURPLE

Purple is a cool cup of blackcurrant juice,
Purple is a blackberry pie,
Purple is the look of a nice juicy plum
And when you eat a lolly,
Purple is the colour of a bright purple tongue.

Laura McDermott (9)
Ouston Junior School

A SPIDER'S LEGS

The first leg is like a narrow, long straw,
The second leg is like a gigantic church spire,
The third leg is like a large lamp post,
The fourth leg is like an enormous string of a kite,
The fifth leg is like an extra large chocolate matchmaker,
The sixth leg is like a huge stick of liquorice,
The seventh leg is like a tall tower,
The eighth leg is like a tall brick wall.

Ben Wilson (8)
Ouston Junior School

THE SPIDER'S WEB

The spider's web is like a beautiful ring glistening in the sunlight,
The spider likes it better than anything else
Because its home is made out of strong, knitted thread,
It's a sticky trap to catch its prey,
The bees and flies are scared to go near the tangled web.

Andrew Ballantyne (8)
Ouston Junior School

THE SPIDER'S WEB

The spider's web is a great home for a spider,
It's a thing of beauty,
It's decorated with tiny water beads,
In the morning, it's like a delicate veil,
It shimmers in the sunlight,
It sparkles in the moon,
Always remember -
It can be a snare or a cage.

Sophie Taylor (8)
Ouston Junior School

IF SPIDERS WERE TEN FEET TALL . . .

If spiders were as big as this,
How small would we seem?
Their legs would be as tall as our schools
And their faces would be huge.
Bears would reach up to the moon
And tower above us like giants.
Imagine a lion's ferocity, we would run for our lives!
Blue whales would cover planet Earth and squash all our people.
Ants would be as big as buses and we would ride on them
And if an ostrich cried, we would think it was raining.
If spiders were as big as this,
How small would we seem?

Charlotte Hogg (8)
Ouston Junior School

GRANDAD

Grandad is brave,
Even though he is stuck in a cave,
With doctors and nurses,
Grandma sitting with her purses,
Grandad has made lots of friends,
While he mends,
The hospital is busy,
Watching it all, he gets dizzy,
Grandad lies in bed,
One of his friends is called Ted,
He has a tube up his nose,
From Grandma he received a rose,
One of the men is a loon,
I hope Grandad gets better soon.

Lauren Jackson (10)
Ouston Junior School

BLACK AND WHITE

Black and white is Newcastle winning the FA Cup
Black and white is what dogs see
Black and white are keys on a keyboard playing their music
Black and white is a chessboard
Black and white is Dalmatian's fur.

Andrew Ellison (8)
Ouston Junior School

THE SPIDER'S WEB

The spider's web is like a tough, strong cage to catch its food,
The beautiful silky thread makes a snare to catch flies,
The glistening web blows in a gale while sticking to the wall,
The web sparkles like jewels in the sunlight,
The knitted home is a delicate tangled web.

Benjamin Mulligan (7)
Ouston Junior School

WINTER

The snow in winter is crunchy,
Soft,
Cold,
White as a polar bear,
Cool,
As cold as the Ice Age,
That's when the ice starts on a frosty day,
Snowmen everywhere.

Michael Fella (9)
Ravensworth Terrace Primary School

My Christmas Poem

The tree, the lights, the tinsel,
All celebrate Christmas time,
Would you at Hullabaloo,
Please read my humble rhyme.

Think about the turkey,
It's eaten up so quick,
It's gone before I get a bite,
Before I get a lick.

Don't forget the presents,
Books and clothes and toys,
Some are for the girls,
Some are for the boys.

What about the crackers,
'Oh, is this for me?'
A toy, a joke, a hat,
The *snap* makes all pets flee.

The food (yum, yum), the presents,
Whatever you like best,
It's been a busy Christmas Day,
I think I'll have a rest.

Jonathan Lloyd (9)
Ravensworth Terrace Primary School

Animals

I like brown dogs running on the beach
I like white polar bears catching fish
I like brown horses eating green grass
I love honey-coloured foxes running about
I like brown bears eating honey
I like golden hamsters eating their food

I like dolphins splashing about
I love squirrels jumping from tree to tree
I like birds that sing
I like blue whales jumping all over
I love animals!

Jordan Fleming (8)
Ravensworth Terrace Primary School

ANIMAL POEM

Ferocious dragons flying in the air,
Hairy bears coming out to scare,
Orange sly foxes running around,
Black and white dogs sitting on the ground,
Cheeky hyenas pulling funny faces,
Fat grey elephants packing up their cases,
Thin blue dolphins swimming happily in the sea,
Hairy orang-utans eating their one last tea.

Tiny ants looking at the plants,
Scary trapdoor spiders looking in your pants!
Green caterpillars staring at the ground,
Lots of red centipedes making such a loud sound,
Beautiful butterflies flying peacefully in the air,
Lots of grizzly bears standing there to stare.

Hairy monkeys going terribly crazy,
Lots of orang-utans going totally lazy,
Stupid, ugly monkeys swinging from side to side,
Hairy gorillas getting chased and trying to hide,
Cute squirrels jumping from branch to branch,
Ugly gorillas swinging from side to side.

Charlotte Bell (9)
Ravensworth Terrace Primary School

SEASONS

Winter's when the snow comes
And all the flowers die
But why winter lasts so long
No one knows why

Spring is when the flowers grow
With colours ever so bright
And all the fruit so ripe and juicy
Winter says bye-bye

Summer is when the sunshine comes to stay
Never fear
So you may as well enjoy all the light
Cos autumn's nearly here

Autumn's when the leaves all turn brown
Red and yellow
So say goodbye to all the pears
So rich, ripe and mellow

Now all the seasons I've told you about
Will come here again
But look out for all the snow
Because winter will soon begin.

Leah Cosgrove (8)
Ravensworth Terrace Primary School

ANIMAL POEM

The white sharks eating all the fish
The killer whales chasing the sharks away
The dolphins diving up and down
The water snakes slither left and right and up and down
The grass snakes and king cobras hiding in the trees and bushes

The rhinos charging into the hills
The dogs barking at the cats
The cats chasing the mice
The giraffes eating all the leaves on the trees
Do you care about animals?

Christopher Cowan (9)
Ravensworth Terrace Primary School

WHAT IS BLUE?

Blue is the colour of a boat,
Blue is the colour of my waterproof coat.
Blue is the water of the sea,
Blue is the key ring of a key.
Blue is the colour of your eye,
Blue is the colour of the sky.
Blue can be ink,
Blue can be the power-aid drink.
Blue is a pencil pot,
Blue is a baby's cot.
Blue can be a balloon,
Blue is the sky around the moon.
Blue can be felt,
Blue can be the rim of a belt.
Blue can be the cover of a book,
Blue can be the apron of a cook.
Blue can be a file,
Blue can be a bathroom tile.
Blue can be a door,
Blue can be the living room floor.
Blue is the teacher's folder,
Blue is our faces when it's colder.

Sara Louise Glen (9)
Ravensworth Terrace Primary School

ALL THE ANIMALS

Dogs
Will dogs still have wet noses
And will they still have sparkling eyes?

Blue whales
Will blue whales still be as big as they are now
And will they still be as friendly as they are now?

Rabbits
Will rabbits still be small
And will they still have long ears?

Fish
Will fish still have fins
And will pet fish still eat fish flakes?

Robin redbreast
Will robins still have red breasts
And will they still tweet their little song?

I wonder?

Sophie Malay Muncaster (8)
Ravensworth Terrace Primary School

ANIMALS

Does anyone care about the animals?
They're mostly like you and me,
They are cute and furry, some live in the sea
How will they survive?

In the future will animals still exist
Or will factories squash their homes?
And will they breathe the fumes from cars?
How will they survive?

In the sea, oil has arrived,
Sharks are being killed for their fins,
Some people are still killing whales,
How will they survive?

Charlotte Lynn (9)
Ravensworth Terrace Primary School

SCHOOL

Ravensworth Terrace is a brilliant school
The teachers are nice
My friend, Gavin, likes mice
Ravensworth Terrace is an excellent place
This school is so good
When we get the ball, our shoes become mud
Ravensworth Terrace - so, so great
Lunchtimes are fun
We come in at quarter-past one
Ravensworth Terrace is a brilliant school
Teachers make themselves clear
My friends have no fear
Ravensworth Terrace is an excellent place
We play hide-and-seek
I know my friends peek
Ravensworth Terrace - so, so great
My friends are the best
But can also be pests
Ravensworth Terrace County Primary School
The best one to wish for
It is so cool.

Derry Barton (10)
Ravensworth Terrace Primary School

FUTURE

Will wild animals still roam free?
Will there even be one tree?
In the future.

Will roads cover glens?
Will there still be tiny wrens?
In the future.

Will fruits still be ripe?
Will there be miles of pipe?
In the future.

Will elephants still exist?
Will exhaust fumes make a mist?
In the future.
What will happen?
Who knows?

Nicola Jane Carter (9)
Ravensworth Terrace Primary School

THE SUN!

The sun is a golden eye,
That shuts when the day is done.

The sun is a sizzling chip,
That cooks when the night is gone.

The sun is a giant ball,
That rolls across the sky.

The sun is a sparkly gem,
So darkness say *bye-bye!*

Carmel Woolmington (9)
Ravensworth Terrace Primary School

THE LORD'S ANIMALS

Will the Lord's animals still exist?
Will savage lions, tigers, leopards still have meat?
Will the clicky zebras still have stripes?
Will the spotty jaguars still climb?
Will the sprinty cheetahs still be fast?
Will rude chimpanzees still jump around?
Will bears still roar?
Will deer still butt?
Will snakes bite?
Will fat elephants still eat?
Will spiders scare you?
Will hedgehogs still have spikes?
Well, I hope they will.

Lee Alcock (8)
Ravensworth Terrace Primary School

THE SEASONS

Winter snow is white and fluffy,
Winter is cold and breezy,
Winter is a big block of ice,
Spring is where the buds shoot out,
Spring is where the beautiful yellow daffodils sprout,
Spring is beautiful,
Summer is hot, hot, hot
And hotter than hot but you will like squirting water guns,
Autumn is when the leaves turn gold, orange and red,
But sometimes you know when autumn is here.
Wow! Wow! Wow!

Callum Farrage (9)
Ravensworth Terrace Primary School

THE SEASONS

Spring is the season that starts in March
With the buds on the trees and the newborn animals

Summer is the season that's after spring
With the hot blazing sun, now the trees are green

Autumn is the season after summer
With the red, brown and gold leaves
And the crunching under my feet when I walk

Winter is the season after autumn
With no leaves on the trees and the snow falls slowly down
Or hard like a blizzard in the South Pole.

Connor Rogerson (9)
Ravensworth Terrace Primary School

WINTER, WINTER, WINTER!

Will winter have snowflakes fall on Christmas?
Will children ever throw a single snowball?
Will winter ever have snow?
Will an adult enjoy snow?
Will winter ever go away
And summer come today?
Will winter just give up
And a child say, 'Look up!'?
Winter says, 'Bye-bye.'

Lauren Malloy (8)
Ravensworth Terrace Primary School

ALL GOD'S ANIMALS

Sharks swimming gracefully in the deep blue sea,
Whilst dolphins sing their song,
Bunnies jumping over the green grass,
These are all God's animals.

Polar bears white as snow,
Penguins playing on the ice,
Snowflakes falling from the sky,
Emperor penguins looking so grand,
These are all God's animals.

Butterflies that flutter by,
Robin redbreast,
Swallow, black and graceful,
So just take a minute and think awhile,
These are all God's animals!

Amy O'Mara (8)
Ravensworth Terrace Primary School

ANIMAL POEM

Big, hairy gorillas,
Sitting on a branch.
Tall bears ready to pounce.
Blue whales ferociously biting shrimps' bums,
Will there be anymore sharks left?
Ferocious lions chewing up their dinner,
Copycat parrots saying what you are.
Jumping kangaroos chasing you,
Silly monkeys playing tricks on you.

Joshua Gray (8)
Ravensworth Terrace Primary School

A CHEETAH

A cheetah has bright golden skin
Dark brown spots between its golden skin

It moves like a dog running for its life
Its speed is like a motorbike's top speed in a race

It takes its prey down quietly to eat it
People are killing these great animals for their skin
And they're becoming extinct every minute we speak.

Sean Starmer (9)
Ravensworth Terrace Primary School

THERE'S A MONSTER IN MY WARDROBE

Sometimes at night
I hear things in my wardrobe
Like scratching and banging
It's almost like they're coming in
Sometimes I hide under my quilt
Scared stiff and shaking
Then I hear more
Scratching and banging
I hear things in my wardrobe
When I wake up, my wardrobe door is open
I look in but nothing's there
When I get to bed again
I see a big yellow tooth almost
The size of my hand
There's something in my wardrobe
And I think it's a monster.

Craig Turnbull (10)
Raventhorpe Preparatory School

FIRE

I was in the dark
And saw smoke,
I went to see what was there,
I saw flickers of little light,
Suddenly it grew bigger and bigger,
It grew even wilder till it was alive.
The colour was great,
All the reds and yellows.
It was noisy enough with all
The crackling, sizzling, roaring.
Then the fire brigade came
And told them, 'Don't come here again!'

Hannah Hillary (10)
Raventhorpe Preparatory School

RED

Red is the colour of autumn leaves
And my red spotted handkerchiefs.
Red is the sign of danger,
Red are the chillies which you use to flavour.
Red are the poppies in the cornfields,
Red is the colour of the apple peel.
Red is the colour of the bed in which I lie,
Red are the plums in my favourite pie.

Olivia Richardson (11)
Raventhorpe Preparatory School

If I

If I ruled the world
Instead of Her Majesty
I am sure my family would visit me
I would be busy every day
No, that wouldn't be me

If I was a tree
It would be very boring for me

If I was a sailor
I would probably be
Seasick all the time
So I can't choose what I want to be
Can you?

Victoria Richardson (9)
Raventhorpe Preparatory School

Weather

Today the weather is windy,
The wind is going through the letter box,
Making it bang.
Now it's starting to rain, it's getting worse,
Now it's starting to rain on the window pane,
Now it's turning to hail.
What a clatter on the windowpane,
Now it's getting even worse,
It's becoming a hurricane.
Finally, it's the end of the day
And all the wind and rain has gone away.

Victoria Whitaker (9)
Raventhorpe Preparatory School

SUPER MAX

I have a dog
He is small, cute and black
But sometimes when he's naughty
My mum shouts, 'I'm going to take him back!'
He loves to run, he loves to roam
But he has a naughty habit
Sometimes on the riverbank
He rolls in a dead fish or rabbit
He cries and frets
When he's home alone
He's not even happy if you leave him a juicy bone
So he has to stay with Grandad, our doggy-sitter
He's good company for Grandad and Max likes it too
But he loves to come home to a big bowl of food
Then lay by the fire
I love my dog.

Samantha Hopper (9)
Raventhorpe Preparatory School

PETS

Pets can be big or small,
They come in all shapes and sizes,
Short, fat, thin or hairy.
Some of them can be quite scary,
They all need food, water, love and care
And with my sister, I must share.
Our hamster, Spice, is greedy and trouble,
One of these days he'll pop like a bubble!

Simon Warne (8)
Raventhorpe Preparatory School

THERE ARE MONSTERS UNDER MY BED

All the monsters come out at night,
They play quiet music,
Not forgetting the disco light
And they will dance to celebrate,
I do not know why.
But one night I got out of bed,
I looked under my bed,
I saw a trapdoor,
I opened the door with a creak,
I opened it a little bit more to have a little peek,
I opened the door and guess what I saw . . . ?

Adam Matthews (9)
Raventhorpe Preparatory School

COLOUR

Blue is the colour of the sky at night
Blue is the colour of my disco light
Blue is the colour of the crashing ocean
Blueberry is the smell of my hair lotion

Yellow is the colour of the sun
And also the colour of the icing on my bun
Yellow is the colour of my bathroom wall
And also the colour of my favourite ball.

Danielle Connelly (10)
Raventhorpe Preparatory School

FIRE

Walking in the dark
All alone in the wood
Suddenly a spark!
Moving swiftly like a snake
Burning hot, orange, gold and red
Creeping up a tree
It reaches the leaves
What can I see?
A dragon capturing a tree
Fire everywhere
Boom!
Chasing me . . .
Jumping from tree to tree
Then the brigade come to save the day
Lucky me!

Jamie Kilday (10)
Raventhorpe Preparatory School

FIRE

The small glowing light
Flickering in the night
Travelling and lighting like a train on a rail
Leaving a glowing trail
Growing with the breeze
Gobbling all the leaves
A killing machine
Eating everything
Burning everything in sight
Burning, burning into the night.

Jonathan Sayer (11)
Raventhorpe Preparatory School

FIRE

In the darkness of the night,
I smelt something that gave me a fright.
Curly smoke came from a pile of leaves,
Little sparks flickering,
A wisp of wind here and there.
A flame I thought I saw.
Here there came a pair
Of very dangerous flames.
They caught a tree . . . up it went,
Into flames, getting bigger and bigger.
In the cold dark night,
Spreading through the air,
I ran.
When I came back . . .
It was too late.
Everything was ruined,
With the roaring of the fire,
Fighting with the roaring wind,
Here was hopefully the end . . .
The rain.

Georgina Williamson (11)
Raventhorpe Preparatory School

MY FAMILY

My mum is bossy,
My dad is not,
My sister is annoying,
Like my brother, Tot.

My grandma is playful,
My grandad is bald
And those two
Are very old.

My budgies are static,
My fish is bad,
My dog is fat,
My cat is mad.

That is my family -
Like it or not,
We together are *h-o-t*
Hot!

Jessica Harland (10)
Raventhorpe Preparatory School

MULTICOLOURED

Pink is the blossom
That blooms on the trees,
Pink is the handkerchief
That catches your sneeze.

Blue is the salty
Wavy sea
And blue is the night sky
Don't you agree?

Green is the tall grass
In the field and meadow,
Green is an alien
Friend or foe.

Yellow is the lemon
On which we dine
And yellow are the rays
Of the golden sunshine.

Amy Matthews (10)
Raventhorpe Preparatory School

FIRE

I'm walking in the park
Alone, in the dark.
There's something wrong here
And it's around me.

I hear trickling and flickering
Flames, smoke and sizzling.
First there is a tiny wisp
Then it grows bigger and bigger.

First I smell smoke,
Then I hear crackling sparks,
Then I see roaring, raging flames,
Then I cry for help.

I turn round and run,
I feel the heat on my back,
It's getting bigger and bigger,
Then it explodes.

Billie-Rae Wilkerson (10)
Raventhorpe Preparatory School

PEOPLE

There're lots of people all over the world,
Some have straight hair, some have curled,
Some have big feet, some are thin,
Some are named Tommy, some are named Lyn.
Some have blonde hair, some have brown,
Some wear a smile, some wear a frown,
Some are bold, some are shy,
Some are funny, some often cry.

Debbie Cheesbrough (10)
Raventhorpe Preparatory School

COLOURS

Pink is the blossom on the trees
Pink is a hanky to catch your sneeze
Pink is the colour of my dress
Pink is the lipstick of a princess

Blue is the colour of the sky
And blue is the colour of a butterfly
Blue is the bottle of my suntan lotion
And blue is the colour of the crashing ocean

Green is the colour of the grape on the vine
Green is the colour of a swaying pine
Green is the colour of the leaves on a tree
Green is the colour of the grass in the lea.

Cheryl Gartland (10)
Raventhorpe Preparatory School

POP STARS

Which one could be my
Favourite
J-Lo, Pink or Nelly?

Which one could be my
Favourite
Westlife, Shaggy or Kylie?

My mum likes Blue
My dad does too
But my favourite is -
Guess who?

Jessica Rushforth (9)
Raventhorpe Preparatory School

TREES

Trees come in different forms
Bendy, twisty and sometimes wonky
Some lose leaves and some keep them
In autumn I like it best
The leaves all turn
Red, yellow and brown
But Christmas trees stay green
All year round.

Harriet Peacock (10)
Raventhorpe Preparatory School

SNOW

Snow is a salt shaker that
   has fallen over from Heaven!
It's dandruff that has been
   shaken off!
It's a shower and all the
   water has frozen in mid-air!
It's clouds sweating in the sun
   for the air to freeze!
It's a cloud with a very
   bad cold!
It's water from the guns
   the gods use for a water fight to fall as snow!
It's a frozen lake that has fallen
   off the side of the Earth!
It's flour from God's giant
   cooking machine!

Thomas Caygill (11)
St Augustine's Primary School, Darlington

THE SEA

The sea is a tiger,
King of all beasts,
He only appears
When the tide is on Neaps

The sea is a lion,
Also a king,
He comes out
When the tide is at spring.

The sea is a rhino,
Ready to charge,
When he roars
The waves turn large.

The sea is a horse,
Pretty and proud,
When he's around
The wind is loud.

The sea is a panda,
Ferocious and wild,
But he can be
Meek as a child.

The sea is an animal,
Big or small,
But I know
That I love them all.

Natasha Redpath (11)
St Augustine's Primary School, Darlington

WHAT IS THE MOON?

The moon is a big piece of cheese
Which God eats

It is a big football in the air
Being kicked

It is a big, white, delicious birthday cake
Covered in icy sugar

It is a really big snowball
Being thrown in the air.

Matthew Morgan (10)
St Augustine's Primary School, Darlington

RHINO

R   is for rare species
H   is for hunted, poachers hunt them down
I   is for intelligent the rhino is
N   umbers of them have been killed
O   ther species are rare as well.

Ciar Purser (11)
St Augustine's Primary School, Darlington

MY FRIENDS!

Some are small
The others are tall
When we fall
We help each other
But we stay cool together!

My friends are the best
Better than the rest
My friends are cool
We go to the same school
My friends are the best!

Lisa Thornton (11)
St Augustine's Primary School, Darlington

HARVEST TIME

The fields of corn are golden, inland beaches.
The pears are gold and green treasure.
The apples are emeralds and rubies,
The haystacks are sun-coloured mountains,
The sacks of potatoes are delicious heavyweights,
The loaves of bread are tanned hills of taste,
The richness of the smell is as rich as roses,
The happiness is so great, you can almost taste it.

Jonathan Lumsdon (11)
St Augustine's Primary School, Darlington

A TIGER

A tiger is a fire,
    red and orange stripes, flaming hot in our eyes.
A tiger is an orange and yellow ball,
    ready to bounce on us.
A tiger is paint,
    different shades mixed together.
A tiger is our king
    and the king of the jungle.

Emma Spraggon (10)
St Augustine's Primary School, Darlington

MY HORSE

My horse is the best, my horse is brill,
But when we ride, we go with the flow.

My horse is brown, with lovely blue eyes
And his hooves as muddy as pigsties.

He's lovely and sweet with rosy cheeks
And his best friend is me, like me to him.

My horse is well behaved, with me on his back,
Will win first prize wherever we go.

When mucking out, I tie him up,
Naughty and mischievous and sometimes he escapes.

I groom him nicely, shiny and glistening,
His coat as smooth as silk.

I see him nearly every day,
With those big eyes you can't say no to him.

So give him a carrot,
My horse is lovely, Benji.

Helen Richardson (11)
St Augustine's Primary School, Darlington

KIDS

K ids, why do they always get so muddy?
I   don't know what to do with them!
D o they always keep on growing?
S   o what is the purpose of kids?

Bianca Fawlk (10)
St Augustine's Primary School, Darlington

WITNESSES

The bees were a witness, many of them feared
As soon as he had come, the man had disappeared
He seemed like a race, gone without trace
The eagles were a witness, swooping in the sky
Whilst he himself wished he could fly
Again he had gone, blazing like the sun
The foxes were a witness, hidden in the trees
Whilst he himself, scowled at the leaves
Off he went with his back bent
The children were a witness, playing with a ball
Watching in horror as he began to fall
He had gone, never to return
And the things which had seen him, fled in turn.

Leo Logan Cassidy (10)
St Augustine's Primary School, Darlington

CARS FOR ME

C ars, a creation for speed
A fine work of art, for I hope the engine will start
R acing and rally, touring, all are good for me
S uspension and sideboards and nice tail wings

F lying along at high rate of speed
O rienteering all by itself, better than any man's steed
R evelation speed, everything I need or want

M ore cars, more excitement, more fun!
E ventually it's time to leave the leather seats
    For a wooden chair because it's time to eat.

Joss Klein (11)
St Augustine's Primary School, Darlington

IN THE SNOW

In the snow, in the snow
Is it slush or is it ice?
Is it ice or will it melt?
Is it cold or just OK?
Is there enough to build a snowman?
Will it last the rest of the day?
Can I go and have my lunch?
I think I'll go, I'm sure it will last
Yum, yum, it's my favourite
But the sun's come out
There it goes, my snowman . . .
Gone!

Katharine Murphy (11)
St Augustine's Primary School, Darlington

THE BEACH

The beach is an ear
Lying on its side

The sea is a sound
Going up the ear

The jungle is hair
Just behind the ear

The sand is the skin
Never moves, never makes a sound

The people on the beach
Are hairs on the ear.

Andrew Wynne (10)
St Augustine's Primary School, Darlington

CREATURES AND ANIMALS

C is for cow, calm in a field of green grass,
R is for rabbit, running through a field of tall grass,
E is for elephant, eating all it can,
A is for ants accruing on a pathway,
T is for Tigger, timing his pounce,
U is for underwater, where lots of animals live,
R is for rats, racing each other down in the drains,
E is for elephant, stamping in the grass,
S is for snake, slithering all around.

Hayley Eccles (10)
St Augustine's Primary School, Darlington

THAT DOG

T hat dog is white and brown, he has no mind
H e remembers his manners, he's quite
A softie, he loves his belly rubbed
T hat dog happens to be my dog

D exter's his name, sleeping his game
O h, if only he could fetch
G oing to sleep again.

Robert Corless (10)
St Augustine's Primary School, Darlington

ART

     A rt is good fun, it makes me run with joy
a   R t, we can draw, paint, sketch and even shade
but T he best thing of all is sticking and gluing,
       design and choose paint with care.

Danny Smith (10)
St Augustine's Primary School, Darlington

MY HORSE

My horse is like a sandy beach
covered in sand from head to toe

His tail goes swish
like a palm tree waving in the wind

His name is Magic
and he's as magical as a magician

Magic loves to jump in the field
like a frolicking lamb in the spring

He can never wait to go outside
like a child at Christmas

Magic loves apples
like a child with candy

But above all, my horse is always good
like a child in a sweet shop.

Emma Mitchell (10)
St Augustine's Primary School, Darlington

FOOTBALL

F   ootball, now that's a goal
O   ver every single match there is always a goal
O   h no, it is not rare to score in every single match
T   ut tut tut, that's a bad foul, red card, you're off
B   oring, you should not have done that
A   t three o'clock, it is kick-off time
L   ook at that, it was a good goal
L   ook again, was it offside?

Sean Simpson (10)
St Augustine's Primary School, Darlington

ANIMALS IN THE SEA

Octopuses have eight arms,
They are very, very long,
Fish make a funny sound,
Like they're singing a song.

Starfish are very bumpy,
They are very pink,
Sharks have very big teeth,
But they hardly ever blink.

Dolphins have very good hearing,
They can always catch their prey,
Wales are very big,
They always get their own way.

Animals in the sea,
They get on very well,
They are all good friends,
Does that ring a bell?

Emma Galbraith (10)
St Augustine's Primary School, Darlington

DOLPHINS

D   olphins are mammals that jump high above
O   ver and under the water they go
L   oving, caring mammals, they swim with the flow
P   hillippa, my auntie, loves them so
H   orrible people try to kill them, so please look after them
I   n England there are hardly any!
N   one, apart from the ones in tanks!
S   o please help them live in peace and harmony!

David McGovern (11)
St Augustine's Primary School, Darlington

RABBITS

My rabbits are nice and sweet
Not like my dad's smelly old feet
I see them almost every day
When I come home from school
And go out to play
I have three in all
Two girls and a boy
And I could cuddle them all
Like my favourite toy
My favourite rabbit is one called Daisy
She lives with three guinea pigs
And she drives them crazy.

Anna Barnes (10)
St Cuthbert's RC Primary School, Crook

ANIMALS

Animals are all around
Sometimes they make lots of sound
Like my dog, Bess
Who can make lots of mess

They can be as small as a mouse
Or as big as a house
They can have lots of hair
But I don't care
Because I like animals and that is that.

Philipa Donaghue (11)
St Cuthbert's RC Primary School, Crook

CATS

Cats are cute, as cute as can be,
I have two that belong to me.
When I come into the house
They always have a little mouse.
One is black,
One is grey,
They are both cute, as cute as can be.

Natalie Poulter (10)
St Cuthbert's RC Primary School, Crook

EVIL AND KINDNESS

Evil is red like the Devil's horns and tail
It smells like fire like off the end of the Devil's tail
It tastes like meat like the Devil's favourite food
It sounds like the chant of war, the Devil's favourite sound
It feels like burning, inside the Devil burns the fire
Evil lives in us all

Kindness is white
It smells like strawberries
It tastes like sugar cane
It sounds like a bird
It feels like water
It lives in sweet summer.

Bridget Harrison (8)
St Joseph's RC Primary School, Durham

PEACE AND WAR

Peace is lilac
It smells like perfume
Tastes like whipped cream
Sounds like the sound of laughter
Feels like the spikes on hedgehogs
Lives in the heart of Saturn

War is brown
It smells of rotten salad
Tastes like bitter vinegar
It sounds like rain pouring down
Feels like lava going through your hand
War lives in the middle of an earthquake.

Thuy Pham Thi Minh (9)
St Joseph's RC Primary School, Durham

HOPE AND WAR

Hope is the colour red
It smells of the juiciest fruit
It tastes of the best strawberries
It feels like someone tickling
Lives in the heart of an angel

War is the colour black
It smells of rotten cheese
It tastes like mud
It sounds like a gunshot
It feels like someone punching me
Lives in the heart of a volcano.

Ben Newton (9)
St Joseph's RC Primary School, Durham

LOVE AND HATE

Love is the colour yellow
Love smells of daffodils in a summer's breeze
Also it tastes like sweets
And it sounds like the ice cream van's music
It feels as soft as a sponge
And it lives in the core of our hearts

Hate is the colour black
Hate smells like burnt rabbit
And it tastes like mud
Also it sounds like madness
It feels like lava
And it lives in the heart of Hell.

Joe Hoban (9)
St Joseph's RC Primary School, Durham

WAR AND PEACE

War
The colour is dark black, like a cave
It smells like a rotten egg
It tastes like mouldy cheese
Sounds like someone getting murdered
You feel pain
It lives in a castle

Peace
The colour of peace is orange
It smells like a cup of tea
It sounds like somebody laughing
It lives in church.

Liam Scollen (8)
St Joseph's RC Primary School, Durham

HAPPINESS AND SADNESS

The colour of happiness is bright, bright yellow
The smell is as strong as flowers
The taste is as scented as tea leaves
The sound is a happy merry-go-round
The feel of a smooth silk cloth
The home of all this is the beach, far away.

Sadness is grey
The smell of coal
Drinking cold tea . . . horrible taste
The sound of an empty tin dropping from high
The feel of a rough stone
And it lives in a burning building.

Laura Scotter (9)
St Joseph's RC Primary School, Durham

LOVE AND HATE

Love is the colour red
It smells like strawberries and cream
It tastes very sweet
It sounds like tinkling sugar
It feels very soft
And it lives inside my heart

Hate is the colour grey
It smells like burning
It tastes like burnt sausages
It sounds like crackling on a barbeque
It feels very hard
And it lives in the air.

Georgia Lincoln (9)
St Joseph's RC Primary School, Durham

PEACE AND WAR

Peace is the colour of bright blue
Peace smells of pollen
Peace tastes of fresh white bread
Peace sounds like birds singing in the summer
Peace feels like soft silk
Peace lives in hearts of kindness

War is the colour red
War smells of wet dog
War tastes of fire
War sounds like explosions
War feels sharp
War lives in the heart of Hell.

Mark Hunter (9)
St Joseph's RC Primary School, Durham

WAR AND PEACE

War is crimson
Smells like a public toilet
Tastes like a rotten egg
Sounds like a cannon going off
Feels like fire
War lives in a twister

Peace is white
Smells like melted chocolate
Tastes like ice cream
Sounds like birds singing
Feels like a cloud
Peace lives in a rainbow.

Richard Misiak (9)
St Joseph's RC Primary School, Durham

HOPE AND DESPAIR

Hope is the colour white shining in the dark night
It smells like summer flowers in the breeze
Hope tastes like soft chocolate ice cream
It sounds like early birds singing in the trees
Hope feels like winning the lottery
Hope lives in your mind

Despair is the colour dark green
Despair smells like sweaty socks in the oven
Despair tastes like mouldy cheese in the fridge
Despair sounds like people screaming
Despair feels like death
Despair lives in back alleys and tight bin bags.

Joseph Hirst (9)
St Joseph's RC Primary School, Durham

LOVE AND HATE

Love is orange
It sounds like a piano playing in motion
It tastes like wind swaying along the grass
It smells like curry cooking
It feels like hot sunshine burning in the sky
Love lives in your heart and lips

Hate is black
It smells like coal melting
It tastes like anger and sadness
It sounds like old memories
It feels like wind breezing
Hate lives in the mine.

David Hopper (9)
St Joseph's RC Primary School, Durham

HAPPINESS AND SADNESS

Happiness is the colour of purple
It smells like the outside world when its sunny
It's a similar taste to ice cream
The feel of it is my favourite toy
The sound of it is a group of people laughing
It lives all round my family

Sadness is the colour of blue
It smells like dirty mud
It tastes like ordinary water
The feel of it is a hard rock
The sound of it is raindrops falling to the ground
It lives in everyone's house.

Caitlin Scullion (8)
St Joseph's RC Primary School, Durham

WINTER

I love snow,
I like building snow because it is winter.

I like catching snowflakes on my tongue,
Because it is winter.

I like snowball fights because it is winter.

I like black ice because it is winter.

I like snowdrops because it is winter.

I like sledging because it is winter.

It happens, it happens each winter.

Jade Pearson (8)
St Teresa's RC Primary School, Darlington

I LOVE WINTER

I can see the frost on the windows
I can touch the snow and I can make snowmen
I wear my hat and gloves
I like to see the frost
It's such a nice sight
I open my Advent calendar
I light my winter candles
The leaves are off the trees
Disappeared and gone
I like winter so much.

Thomas Bell (7)
St Teresa's RC Primary School, Darlington

WINTER

Winter is good,
People throw snowballs in winter,
Sometimes they land in their mouths,
I can see frost on the windows,
They are icy and cold-looking.

Ryan Thorns (7)
St Teresa's RC Primary School, Darlington

CHRISTMAS HAIKU

Santa is coming
Santa is bringing presents
He is on the roof.

Joe Hewitt (10)
St Teresa's RC Primary School, Darlington

THE BEST BITS OF WINTER

Winter's frosted lily-white wings flap down on the land,
They cover the rabbits' front door and the ducks' lake.
The lake looks like a mirror reflecting the landscape.
The spiders' webs are shown for the snow lays on them,
Looking like diamond lace.
The Christmas trees, bare as a backbone, stick out like sore thumbs.

James Smith (11)
St Teresa's RC Primary School, Darlington

WINTER

One day in the park on a midwinter's day
When the snow was deep and crisp
Not a sound could be heard
No footprints
Just me and a white, empty park
All the animals tucked up in bed
Dreaming sweet dreams.

Thomas Manning (8)
St Teresa's RC Primary School, Darlington

BRIGHT NIGHT

It's Bonfire Night, oh what a sight
Guy Fawkes died on this bright night
Fireworks are blazing up into the sky
Quick move out the way or you might die
The fireworks' ash is as dull as death
Everyone gasps and holds their breath.

Christopher Thomas Ward (10)
St Teresa's RC Primary School, Darlington

AUTUMN BREEZE

A soft cool breeze runs through the air,
Slowly moving the trees side to side.
Raindrops fall but nobody minds,
Kids play on, no care in the world.
Like a machine on and off, the rain just stops,
But when the sun goes down, the kids start to slow.
Like kids in a candy store no more.
The wind turns colder, the breeze turns harder.
The kids and all the other kids,
Lie safe in their nice comfy beds.

Michael Holmes (11)
St Teresa's RC Primary School, Darlington

AUTUMN

Showers of brown, orange and yellow,
Autumn time has just begun,
Summer has gone far away,
People playing conkers every day.

Autumn time is very fun,
But the bare-armed trees look very glum,
All the leaves are on the floor,
People crunching on them annoys the trees even more.

Jack Doherty (11)
St Teresa's RC Primary School, Darlington

AUTUMN

Red, orange, yellow and brown,
They never ever make me frown.
Leaves have changed their colour too,
They make us feel so nice and new.

Conkers fall and they have a fight,
To see who is the best.
In the end it starts to snow,
Then I have a nice, warm home to go to.

Rachel Bell (10)
St Teresa's RC Primary School, Darlington

MIDSUMMER EVENING

The shade of orange sun, sets upon crooked park
Bulldogs bark and bark
Green shaded grass covers the rough, rigid concrete
Sounds of the swing slowly swaying
Squeak, squeak, squeak

The smell of sewage fills the drifting air
Spirits of children play, do they dare?
Midsummer evening dawns upon crooked park
Squeak, squeak, squeak!

Megan McSherry & Aisha Shariff (10)
St Teresa's RC Primary School, Darlington

BRIGHT NIGHT!

Guy Fawkes night is such a treat,
I love the colours that fill the street,
The booms, the bangs, the sparks that fly,
Like glitter falling from the sky,
The fireworks go up,
Like little metallic cups.

I love Guy Fawkes night, I always will,
The colours give me such a thrill.

Gabrielle McKenna (11)
St Teresa's RC Primary School, Darlington

SEASONAL WEATHER

Spring is wet,
Wet like a river,
So in the end
It makes me shiver.

Summer is warm,
The temperature is high,
The sun stays out
In the empty sky.

Autumn leaves crashing,
Falling off trees,
I wish it was summer,
Change it, God, please!

Winter is cold,
The sun is love,
Building snowman parents
In the freezing snow.

Michael Thurloway (10)
St Teresa's RC Primary School, Darlington

THE MONSTER'S CAVE

A big, green, mean gigantic troll with a ginormous hard stick
A long red lake of human blood
Trickling water running down the wall and dripping off the stony roof
A long, deep, dark cave
Smelly
With black
A tube-shaped cave
Quiet
Shadows on the wall.

Kieran Elliot (8)
St Teresa's RC Primary School, Darlington

THE WITCH'S CUPBOARD

Smelly frogs' legs
And rotting eggs,
Strange spells from distant lands,
Grey dust
And wands that are bust,
A cauldron as black as night,
Empty jars,
Tickets to mud spas,
Wooden spoons as old as the hills,
Magic powder,
Signs that say louder,
Evil potions that'll make you pass out,
Silly chants
And snails from France,
Fretting plots that will end the world.

Jessica Addison (8)
St Teresa's RC Primary School, Darlington

THE GIANT'S HOUSE

Look in through the rocky gates
Be quiet as a mouse
We're going to sneak and take a peek
Inside the giant's house
Look inside the rusty bedroom
Look, look, look and you'll see
I will frighten thee
Look inside, inside and you will see
That one day, one day this will be your dream.

Ashleigh Moss (8)
St Teresa's RC Primary School, Darlington

THE MONSTER'S CAVE

Pools of pure human blood left from the monster's lunch,
Stalactites and stalagmites dripping with human blood
Where the monster killed him,
Bones shattered on the floor in no certain order,
Bits of ripped clothing lying on the floor,
Then I looked at my feet and I daren't move anymore,
I ran out of the cave and forgot about the things I'd seen,
The monster disappeared and I'd forgot about the things I'd seen.

Charlotte Foster (8)
St Teresa's RC Primary School, Darlington

AUTUMN BREEZE

A soft wind in the sky,
Blowing the leaves up high.

Standing for conkers we are under a tree,
Mind your head, *oh no*, it's coming for me.

The days start early, the nights are dark,
Hallowe'en is coming, a time for a lark.

Stuart Watson (11)
St Teresa's RC Primary School, Darlington

SCHOOL

At school you might eat turkey,
At school you might eat toast,
At school you might feel perky,
At school you might just boast.

At school it might be easy,
At school it might be hard,
At school you might be teasy,
At school you might have a mard.

Rebecca Bates (7)
St Teresa's RC Primary School, Darlington

THE ALIEN SPACESHIP

In a spaceship the alien lurks, waiting for somebody to come
Close to *jump* out and get them, to suck their blood.

The alien has a large body for when he gets you in his tummy, but
don't come close because he's waiting to *jump* out and get them to suck
their blood.

The alien has a big sloppy mouth for when he eats you, don't come
close because he's waiting to *jump* out and get you to suck your blood.

Mark James Anderson (8)
St Teresa's RC Primary School, Darlington

THE MONSTER'S CAVE

Monsters, ugly, smelly and stinky
Skeletons, old, hanging on the door
Dungeon, gooey
Gigantic monsters, large and frightening
Spiderwebs, sticky
Bits of ripped clothing
Purple spots on the monster
Dark, spooky cave.

Mandeep Uppal (8)
St Teresa's RC Primary School, Darlington

FAIRY GROTTO

Berries in acorn bowls
Money trees planted in white plant pots
A golden throne stands in the corner
Tree stumps stand near the wall
Fairies go flying with sparkling wings
Leaves laying on the dusty ground
Flowers growing everywhere.

Lauren Wilthew (8)
St Teresa's RC Primary School, Darlington

THE GIANT'S CASTLE

There's human blood puddles where he has bitten them,
There is one called Judy and one called Ben.
There are monsters all around,
But they are not very loud.
Skeletons hanging on the door,
Mice running on the floor.

Abbi Sheriff (8)
St Teresa's RC Primary School, Darlington

WINTER

We like sledging in the cold snow
I feel warm in my furry coat and gloves
My nose turns cold and I look like Rudolph.

Haydn McKenna (7)
St Teresa's RC Primary School, Darlington

The Monster's Cave

In the hilly mountain
There is a monster cave
Don't go in or you will die!
There is a man in a hole with moth's blood
Most people fall with a really big thud
Cave paintings on the wall
Don't press the button or a bug will fall
Dead bodies on the floor
Ripped to pieces by the beast
The rope looks like plaits
Oh no, the beast has seen me,
No!

Ryan Kindred (8)
St Teresa's RC Primary School, Darlington

Christmas Is Coming

Outside is fun time,
With snowmen and snowballs,
There is lots of fun,
Presents are coming,
Reindeer are flying,
They will soon be arriving,
It is Christmas Day
And sleigh bells are ringing,
Which means Santa's been,
For Christmas dinner
It's turkey and gravy,
So eat up and have fun.

Amanda Walker (10)
St Teresa's RC Primary School, Darlington

SILVER SWIMMER

A deep-sea diver,
An ever survivor.

A cruel hunter,
A punter to poach.

A move topic,
A blue sea liver.

A razor mouth,
A lover of the south.

A catalogue to make me a . . .
Shark.

Jade Watson (11)
St Wilfrid's RC VA Primary School, Bishop Auckland

LIGHTNING

A thrashing spear
A supersonic sound
A wrecking machine
A target spotter
A sparkling light
A portrait of fire
A thunderous beast
A pin pointer

A catalogue to make me . . .
Lightning.

Philip Johnson (11)
St Wilfrid's RC VA Primary School, Bishop Auckland

A CAR

A car can be my best friend,
Forever waiting at my command.

A car is a bull roaming from street to street.

It is a taxi to take me from A to B.

A car can be as bright as the sun
And as dull as rain clouds.

Out of town like a cheetah,
In town like a snail.

A car is an arrow shooting to its target.

Keiron Tague (10)
St Wilfrid's RC VA Primary School, Bishop Auckland

CHICKEN

A seed lover
A net hater
A morning caller
A scaredy pants
A cage liver
A shed lover
A bad fighter
A feathered friend

A catalogue to make me a . . .
Chicken.

Jonathon Wright (10)
St Wilfrid's RC VA Primary School, Bishop Auckland

THE BEACH

Stretched out sleepily in the shade
On a day when the sun is as fierce as a lion
I'm feeling really hot and sticky
And my face is as red as a tomato
The sea looks like a blue blanket
As I head towards it for a swim
But the sand burns my feet like hot coal
Making me run as fast as a cheetah
I'm so glad to reach the water
I splash about like an octopus
The tiny waves welcome me like my bed
And I feel as soft as feathers.

Shelby Ballan (11)
St Wilfrid's RC VA Primary School, Bishop Auckland

CHRISTMAS THANK YOUS

Dear Nanny,
Thank you for the DVD, ,The Dragon Slayer,
I'm sure I'll watch it as soon as Dad buys the player.

Dear Dad,
Thank you for the deodorant, it's nice of you to think
That the smell of summer roses would take away the stink.

Dear Auntie,
Thank you for the teapot which came without a spout
It's easy to put the water in but I can't get my tea out.

Emma Quinn (10)
St Wilfrid's RC VA Primary School, Bishop Auckland

A MAN OF NATURE

A silent mover
A graceful glider

A wild wind
A battle fighter

A high jumper
A fast rider

A man of nature
A fast racer

A bucking bronco
A fierce mustang

A catalogue to make me a . . .
Horse.

Inkie Ralph (10)
St Wilfrid's RC VA Primary School, Bishop Auckland

NUCLEAR MISSILE

An Olympic winner
A nuclear missile
A cutting edge dagger
A jumping bloodhound
A fisherman's dinner
A risk taker
A gambling terrorist
What am I?

Shark!

Lewis Wright (10)
St Wilfrid's RC VA Primary School, Bishop Auckland

CHRISTMAS THANK YOUS

Dear Gran,
Thanks for the car.
But I'm too young to ride it by far.
Dad thinks you went mad,
Not meaning to sound bad.
I was well chuffed.
I can't wait till I'm seventeen.

Dear Auntie,
Thanks for the hair gel.
It's going well with Mel.
People say I look like Gareth Gates.
I've got loads of new mates,
It makes all the other boys mad.
It's the best present I've ever had.

Dear Cousin,
Thanks for the slug.
It just sits on my rug.
I've always wanted one,
I thought I'd name him John
But you can pick.
It's so generous of you.

Katie Burge (11)
St Wilfrid's RC VA Primary School, Bishop Auckland

A CROCODILE

It's a long lizard growling
It's a monster on the prowl
It's huge and it's snappy
And it doesn't mess around!
Its big, foggy eyes will see what's going down

When it hunts, it stays low to the ground
Sometimes you can't find him, where can he be?
I only hope he can't find me!
Or he'll have me for his tea!

Abby Whitworth (10)
St Wilfrid's RC VA Primary School, Bishop Auckland

LAVA

Noisy and wild
I tear through the town
Wearing a bright red dressing gown

Destructive by nature
And destructive by heart
I'll tear all the town apart

Speedy and cunning
I tear down mountains
Burning is my hobby
Destroying is my life
And volcano is my wife

Rumbling and tumbling
I run people over
And leave a trail behind

Living in darkness
And always feeling hot
I leave things to rot

What am I?

Brogan Donnelly (10)
St Wilfrid's RC VA Primary School, Bishop Auckland

A DARK STRANGER

A proud pouncer
A sly sneaker

A shadow hiding
A black jet gliding

As swift as a kite
As black as the night

A life liver
A death giver

A very bad sinner
A killer for dinner

A catalogue to make me a . . .
Panther.

Anna Bentley (11)
St Wilfrid's RC VA Primary School, Bishop Auckland

ROAMER

A street racer
A road tearer

A sharp ripper
A king of speed

An angel from Hell
A free roamer

A catalogue to make me a . . .
Motorbike.

Patrick Hoban (10)
St Wilfrid's RC VA Primary School, Bishop Auckland

FOR SALE

For sale,
One granny,
1923 model,
Good condition for year,
Able to toddle,
Original parts,
She's done well to keep,
That is,
Apart from her teeth.
Grey in colour,
Not a bad runner,
This one with free MOT,
So buy one, get one free!

Adam Oyston (10)
St Wilfrid's RC VA Primary School, Bishop Auckland

SPOTTY DOTTER

A cruel killer,
A race winner.

A cat brother,
A cub mother.

A spotty dotter,
A smooth trotter.

A grass hider,
A Savannah rider.

A catalogue to make me a . . .
Cheetah!

Hayley McClory (11)
St Wilfrid's RC VA Primary School, Bishop Auckland

GRAVESTONES

Here lies the body
of Little Bo Peep
Trampled to death
By a giant sheep

Here lies the body
Of Humpty Dumpty
Fell to the ground
With a bumpedy bumpedy

Here lies the body
Of the unicorn
Stabbed himself
With his golden horn

Here lies the bodies
Of the three blind mice
Bitten to death
Because they had lice.

Lucy Watson (10)
St Wilfrid's RC VA Primary School, Bishop Auckland

LAND LOVER

A high jumper
A fast runner
A land lover
A foot flicker
A grass eater
A hay muncher

A catalogue to make me a . . .
Horse.

Amy Watson (10)
St Wilfrid's RC VA Primary School, Bishop Auckland

An Icicle

An icicle is a glass dagger,
It's a fairy's delicate finger,
It's a window of transparent glass.

An icicle hangs from the ceilings of caves
And in the summer it slowly melts away.

Bethany Kelly (11)
St Wilfrid's RC VA Primary School, Bishop Auckland

A Car

A car is a roaring lion when it starts,
It is a four-wheeled glider.
It is faster than the speed of light at top speed.
It is a super model on wheels,
It is a streak of lightning,
Shining in the dark night sky.
Two beacons glow to show us the way.

Kieran McCormick (11)
St Wilfrid's RC VA Primary School, Bishop Auckland

Great White Shark

Massive,
Feared by man,
All killed by fishermen,
Misunderstood for a killer.

Rare thing.

Keiran Whigham (10)
St Wilfrid's RC VA Primary School, Bishop Auckland

THE IRON MAN

Crash went the Iron Man,
As he stepped off the cliff.
Bang went his legs,
As they fell off.
Bash went his arms,
As they banged off a rock.
Clatter went his hands,
As they scattered all over.
Splash went his ears,
As they landed in the sea.
Tinkle went his eyes,
As they popped out of his head.
Clang went his head,
As it bumped off the rocks.
Was this the end of the Iron Man?

Paige Tully (10)
St Wilfrid's RC VA Primary School, Bishop Auckland

GUESS WHO?

An eagle eye
A child eater
A mini computer
A drum not to be hit
A book reader
A horrible beast
A heart beater
A pulse raiser
A homework maker

A catalogue to make me a . . .
Teacher.

Domonic Bylett (10)
St Wilfrid's RC VA Primary School, Bishop Auckland

RAPPING WITH MARY

Mary had a little lamb
The cutest little thing
Mary's only problem was
That the lamb just could not sing
Mary said, 'I'll have a nap
And think of all good things
Maybe my little lamb will soon
Be a rapping *king!'*

Olyvia Fairless (10)
St Wilfrid's RC VA Primary School, Bishop Auckland

CRUEL SNOW

Silent but deadly like an owl hunting its prey,
A suffocating white blanket spread over the surrounding land,
Hunch-backed branches of trees bend over,
The force of the oncoming snow too heavy,
A bird hopping about on the frozen ground,
Trying to recover a dead worm.
Newborn lambs are not welcomed by this white wilderness.
People are teetering around afraid they might slip.
Cars get stuck, their grip not strong enough
To pull them away from danger.
It drifts from nearby fields covering houses
Like powder being sprinkled.
Everybody is wrapped up protecting themselves
From its evil chill.
Cruel snow.

Niall Cronin (9)
Staindrop CE Primary School

THE RIVER

Silently, smoothly, the clean, shining river cascades down
The outskirts of the small, quiet town,
Delivering water to its thirsty people,
The river's scaly fish swam by as if they were hypnotised
By the river itself, an easy target
For hungry predators.
The river sluggishly moved, carrying useless waste,
Discarded by the public,
It moved onwards, unaware
Of the baby's tiny feet stepping within it,
Or the playful children
Throwing stones in it, no thinking
Forming in their minds.

Dale Gilbert (10)
Staindrop CE Primary School

LEAF FALLING

Brown leaf hung in the mid autumn, waiting to fall
Eventually it started to fall
Slowly
Then the wind caught it and blew it
It started to rock backwards and forwards like a rocking chair
Until it hit the ground gently like a plane landing
It hit a puddle and a drop of water hit the tip of the leaf
Hanging
Motionless
Until one little drop of water jumped off the leaf
Like a bungee-jumper and hit the ground
Like a fierce cheetah pouncing on its prey.

Mark Anthony Humble (10)
Staindrop CE Primary School

SNOW

When you walk on the soft, crisp snow it crackles
Under your feet like a piece of bacon under the grill

When you pick it up, it crumbles in your hands
Make it into a ball and hold it for a long time
Until it turns to ice
When you keep on throwing it, your hands go freezing
When you look at the snow it make you feel cold
It looks like a couple of white sheets of paper
That have never been used for writing or drawing on
Since it's been there.

Matthew Sugden (11)
Staindrop CE Primary School

WINTER

Winter's wind
Moves like a jet of ice,
Snowflakes fall
Like shreds of rice.
In the morning,
Snowballs fly,
Thrown
By children to the sky.
Like a carpet
On the ground,
The snow
Will cover both flat and mound.

Ross Lindsay (9)
Staindrop CE Primary School

WINTER

Winds
Icy winds blow a threatening fear
Down your quivering spine
Like a spider skating on a large
Animated ice rink

Ice
Ice glistening, slippery blanket
Of wet, frosty snow, cold.

Needs
Gloves, warm comforting gloves
Clawing out to pinch your hands,
Hats, woolly, snug hats eating your head,
Scarves reaching out to strangle your chilly neck.

Trees
Snow-bombarded treetops glisten
In the moonlight, sparkling like the
Queen's best jewels.

Earth
All damp, covered in white,
A silky blanket of snow, waiting
For the first footsteps to step and play.

Rain
The rain falls like a cascade of pearls
Dancing through the trees and then shattering into
Golden slithers.

Cara Firmin (9)
Staindrop CE Primary School

SNOW

It lies awake like a beast waiting to pounce
It catches its prey unawares
It has soft feet
Its icy fingers creep in at every gap
It freezes everything in its path
Silently it drifts across the land
Its breath freezes without mercy
People battle against it but in vain
It glares out across the land
Silently it slips away
Soon people emerge
They survey the scene with different views
Some want to get out and play
Others prefer to stay inside
A few are annoyed at the cheek of it
Some just want to get to work
Lots just stay in bed, too tired to be bothered
Some know this is overtime work
Some know this means fun
Soon the sun starts to penetrate it
Finally it is gone
It all runs into the river
We watch it melt sadly
The fun is gone and happiness with it
We trudge home sadly
Knowing that tomorrow will be like every other day
We watch it out of the window
Going, going, gone!

Samuel Fells (9)
Staindrop CE Primary School

WHISPER

Whisper, whisper goes my stupid big sister
To my mum quietly

Whisper, whisper go the flowing trees
Whispering in cold wind, lonely

Whisper, whisper goes the roaring sea
Whispering to the little rocks

Whisper, whisper go the stones
Rattling against smooth, shiny rocks

Whisper, whisper go round secrets
In a large top school

I like the whisper whispering
It's a tune

Sometimes I wish the whispering
Would just *shut up!*

Claire Boyes (10)
Staindrop CE Primary School

THE WIND

Whirling around the wind filled the night,
Waltzing and dancing with the moonlight,
Hands reaching out towards the pitch skies,
There on the ground the lonely wind lies.
Whispering at the trees' wooden bark,
It's voice sweet like a lark
And when the streetlights look down at their feet,
The light glows in the darkness, down in the street.

Amy Heritage (10)
Staindrop CE Primary School

ALL ARE MY FAVOURITE

A stripy tiger,
   A spotty leopard,
      A slippery, slimy snake
      A school of fish
   A killer whale
A wibbly, wobbly jellyfish
A humpy camel
   A scaly lizard
      A straight, spiked cactus
      A cuddly polar bear
   A prancing reindeer
A black and white penguin
A busy mum
   A barking dog
      A yellow tweeting budgie
Are all my favourite things.

Matthew Thompson (10)
Staindrop CE Primary School

WATERFALL

As I sat upon a wall,
I stared down at a waterfall,
There I felt the cold, wet spray,
Gently, as I lay,
Waterfall is raging and roaring,
Like an eagle soaring,
On a beautiful summer's day,
As I sat upon a wall,
I stared down at a waterfall.

Kirsty Davies (10)
Staindrop CE Primary School

FIRE

Yellows, reds and oranges
Dancing in the wind
Warming up my fingers
On a cold winter's night
Men were brushing the cinders
Away from the crowd
As the flames in the fire all went down

Everyone started to move away
When the flickering fire suddenly went out
It walked away from me
My body filled with coldness
My fingers started going numb
As I threw my coat onto the fire
To try and make it burn
My attempt was unsuccessful
The coat did not light
So I walked off into the sunset
On a cold December's night.

Christopher Pearson (11)
Staindrop CE Primary School

FIRE

Burning,
Endless arms of blazing fire.
Destructive,
Destroying anything in its path.
Deadly,
Thick smoke smothering everyone inside.
Violent,
Edging its prey to death.

Michael Boyes (10)
Staindrop CE Primary School

A LONELY WHISPER

A lonely whisper, it bangs my head
Lonely whisper is what I dread
A lonely whisper goes round the door
Lonely whisper under the floor
A lonely whisper goes through my spine
Lonely whisper it isn't mine
A lonely whisper on my nerves
Lonely whisper how it curves
A lonely whisper here we go
A lonely whisper it's sure to say
A lonely whisper's here to stay.

Sarah Thompson (9)
Staindrop CE Primary School

FIRE!

The red burning flames,
  Shout out to the sky.
    Beneath its torturing feet
      The wood crackles out loud
        'Help! Help!'
          It's too late,
          The fire's flames start
        Eating its prey
      Until it dies away
    Its smoky breath dances
As it chokes the night sky
Soon it will die
Like an extinct animal.

Hayd'n Walker (11)
Staindrop CE Primary School

WINTER

The first flurries of snow fall from the white sky,
It clings to the trunks and branches of the trees,
The days get shorter and the nights get longer,
Snowdrops push through the Earth.

Some animals are sleeping,
Some have flown away,
Some are foraging through the snow to find the food,
Scraps are put out for the birds, helping them to survive.

The children are making barricades and having snowball fights
                                    in the streets,
At home, children are toasting their toes on the warm, crackling fire,
The houses looking like igloos under the crisp snow,
The lights flicker in the darkness.

Morning brings the sun again,
Warming up the air,
Slowly the grass appears,
Icicles drip to nothing,
Soon it will be spring and flowers, leaves and insects it will bring.

Peter Bousfield (10)
Staindrop CE Primary School

BRITAIN'S WEATHER

One minute it's sunny
The next minute it's rain
And in a blink of an eye
It changes again

Sometimes you get a shock
As you look out at night
Because the boiling warmth you expected
Has turned into frostbite

The weather people say things
But they never really know
What the weather is going to be
Is it rain or is it snow?

Nathan Nicholson (10)
Staindrop CE Primary School

A STREAM

Still, clear water, looks like glass
With the glinting pebbles in the sunlight
Fringes of grass hanging over the edge
Twigs and branches caught in the cotters

The stream weaves in and out of the trees
Guided by the warm muddy banks
Used by the small ball of fur
That make it their salvational home

Schools of fish swimming upstream
Fighting the current like walking against violent gales
Stopping in a deep pool to take a reset
The sun glints off the silvery scales

The trees stand motionless on the bank
Stretching their limbs over the stream
Standing like guards all tall and straight
Watching over the water as it follows its path

As it travels down through the fields and towns
Endless obstacles in its way
Relentlessly searching for other members of its family
Continuing its never-ending journey.

Josh Wade (11)
Staindrop CE Primary School

My World

My world is nothing like your world,
Mine is dark, cold and gloomy.
Even when I'm jolly and happy,
My feelings stay pitch-black,
I hate the world around me,
Watching it go by.
It's selfish and very unpleasant,
You'll never be able to understand at all,
I'm determined to solve my problem, nobody cares.
So if you ever see me locally,
On my own at the darkest patch,
Just be grateful to be yourself,
My world - nothing like your world.

Philippa Smith (10)
Staindrop CE Primary School

Snow

Snow is the noise of crunching feet,
tumbling across the land.
Snow is blinding bright white,
covering the Earth.
Snow is the feeling of coldness,
melting in your hand.
The never-ending balls of snow,
flying through the air.
Snow is a child's every dream
put into one.
This is why I wish
it would snow every day.

Adam Cansfield (9)
Staindrop CE Primary School

Sat Alone

He sat alone in his ratty chair,
His hair was matted and grey,
All his clothes were ragged and ripped,
For he had pulled at them and made them tear.

His long dusty kitchen was bare,
Except for the old pots and pans,
Which covered the tops of his tables
And if they were dirty he didn't care.

Ashleigh Hewitt (11)
Staindrop CE Primary School

Snow

It glistened lightly in the white moonlight
Like a gold and purple gem
As I stepped slowly into the
Cold white sheet
I froze
Still as solid ice
Death.

Jenny Kirby (10)
Staindrop CE Primary School

Football Crazy

I have a father, he's football mad,
When Newcastle score, he runs around the house like a young lad,
Doing flips and cartwheels all around,
Mother thinks he's quite mad.

Daniel Grainger (11)
Stanley (Crook) Primary School

HULLABALOO

H ere comes the rain,
U mbrellas fly high.
L ittle sun is still to come,
L ittle sun is done.
A cloud of black is coming near,
B ig and bold covering the sky.
A crash of thunder is above,
L ow and high umbrellas swoop.
O ver and under the clouds carry rain,
O n and off the rain will shower,
    but little sun is still to come.

Chelsea Edmundson (10)
Stanley (Crook) Primary School

WINTER

W inter is here
I ce is everywhere
N obody is unhappy
T he New Year has begun
E veryone likes playing in the snow
R ushing winds swoop past.

Amy Martin (10)
Stanley (Crook) Primary School

THE MAN

There is a man called Jackie Chan
Everyone says he's the man
He fights like Bruce, but he is a Chan
He fights evil by night and he does what's right
But he can fight, fight, fight, right in the night

And he can be a kite and in the air he can fight, fight, fight
But everyone says he's as fast as light
But I think he fights just right
He can defend as fast as light
And that is the end of Jackie's night.

Dean Moore (10)
Stanley (Crook) Primary School

MY DOG TARA

My dog Tara
Is small and furry
Her hair is very curly
She likes to go for walks
And plays a very lot
She is always showing her teeth
When she is smiling
She is now quite old
Which is very sad
That is my dog
Taz!

Rachael Littlewood (11)
Stanley (Crook) Primary School

WINTER IS HERE

W ild and cold
I gloos are built
N othing is warm
T he snow is fun
E armuffs on
R oaring blizzards.

Laura Simpson (9)
Stanley (Crook) Primary School

THE DOLPHIN TALE

A s I swim against the current,

D eep below the storm,
O ver I go into a small curl,
L eaping into the air showing my fancy twirl,
P ausing to sing a happy tune,
H appy friends come and join in too,
I swim to Mermaid Bay,
N eeding to feel that a friend is near.

Sara Bell (11)
Stanley (Crook) Primary School

MY KITTENS

K ittens are so cute,
I think they're silly,
T wo of them,
T iny and terrible,
E xpert at playing,
N aughty,
S tupid.

Flora McCabe (10)
Stanley (Crook) Primary School

SCARED

S talking people
C rying loud
A bout the town
R unning wild
E very day
D own town.

Adam Alderson (9)
Stanley (Crook) Primary School

MY DAD

Dad gets up early every morning,
But before he leaves for work -
He comes into my bedroom
To see me.
First he tickles my feet,
Then he tickles my nose,
Then he pulls my covers off me
And tickles me all over,
To make sure I'm awake
And when he comes home from work,
He gives me a *big* hug and asks me
What I've done all day
And then he has a bath,
Afterwards we have a play,
Either with a game or on TV
And when it's time to go to bed,
He tucks me in and kisses me.

Andrew Bell (10)
Shotton Hall Junior School

AUTUMN

Autumn is trees absorbing water from leaves
Autumn is birds flying from country to country
Autumn is leaves with multicoloured patterns on
The ground beneath our feet
Autumn is animals scattering for food before hibernation
Autumn is time for people to start collecting conkers.

Scott Mills (11)
Shotton Hall Junior School

A Day Out At Cragside

As we put our wet bags down,
I was so excited,
To see a huge and charming house,
I was so delighted.

We went into the butler's room,
That was my very best.
We walked round the very big house,
Until we got to the crest.

Then we went to have our dinner,
In the servants' room.
Yummy, yummy, yummy,
In my empty tummy.

After that we were ready
For that power walk,
In that very walk we saw a river,
So we had a power talk.

Before the long power walk,
We went to the shop,
There were lots and lots of stuff,
But I still didn't stop.

Robyn Pallister (10)
Shotton Hall Junior School

Autumn

Conkers falling on the shattering pavement,
The pick of the squirrels feast,
My mam's cooking her home tea,
The football boots of my friend, Lee.

Ross Atkinson (11)
Shotton Hall Junior School

COMPLAINTS

So what, I ripped your book
And burst your ball,
Look,
You can't tell on me,
My complaints are better you see.

Big deal, I snapped your pens,
Then broke your TV,
I've said,
You can't tell on me,
My complaints are better you see.

You can't tell on me,
These are my complaints -
His ball was burst already,
The pencils, snapped before,
The TV shelf - not steady
And I can't take anymore.

Mathew Geldard (10)
Shotton Hall Junior School

AUTUMN COLOURS

Yellow is the sun, unhappy and alone.
Orange is the leaves dodging the wind.
Red is the apples sitting on the trees.
Brown is the trees, crisp and bare.
Gold is the colour that makes it autumn.

Jonathan Scholick (11)
Shotton Hall Junior School

NOVEMBER, A TIME TO REMEMBER

Hallowe'en, the holy evening,
All Saints Day, a time to remember,
All the saints of November,
All Souls Day, the day of November,
To remember the people that died in November,
Guy Fawkes night, the time to remember
The survival of King James in November,
Remembrance Sunday, a time to remember,
The people that died to save November.
Remembrance Day, the time to remember the
People that fought not just in November.

Andrew Westgarth (10)
Shotton Hall Junior School

THE DRAGONS

The dragons are big
The dragons are small
The dragons are coming
Over my wall

People scream and people shout
Telling all and all about
I just stand and close my eyes
People say I'm very wise

But the dragons are big
And the dragons are strong
And now I'm going, going
Gone.

Gemma Scott (11)
Shotton Hall Junior School

GOLDILOCKS AND THE THREE BEARS

Three little bears lived in a wood
Eating porridge for their food
Because it was so very hot
They left it standing in the pot
A little girl came by that way
Her name was Goldilocks they say
She looked into the cottage small
To find it was no marble hall
She tried the porridge in the pots
But found it was very hot
She went upstairs to go to bed
She fell asleep on the smallest bed
Three bears came home
To their cottage small
And ate the porridge one and all
They went upstairs to go to bed
And baby bear cried, 'Look who's in my bed!'
Goldilocks jumped up and fled.

Michelle Burey (10)
Shotton Hall Junior School

AUTUMN

Red is a conker waiting to be picked
Blackberries in the farmyard in the bushes
Squirrels picking its nuts off the tree
Orange leaves falling to the ground
Red apples ready to be picked.

Liam Swift (10)
Shotton Hall Junior School

MY PLANET

My planet Rainmit
Has a huge tropical storm.
With greens and pinks and purples,
Always spreading.
There's a huge pool of acid,
Going across the planet.
There is a UFO,
But my ship is well away.
There's volcanoes and rivers and craters of acid,
That's my planet, *Rainmit!*

Sophie Coldwell (10)
Shotton Hall Junior School

NOVEMBER, A TIME TO REMEMBER

All Saints Day, a time in November,
All Souls Day, the proudest day to remember,
And remember, remember when Guy Fawkes tried to blow up the king,
Remembrance Day is a holy day, not like any other,
Remembrance Sunday, we remember king and country,
One of the saddest days in November.

Scott Westmorland (10)
Shotton Hall Junior School

GREEN IS . . .

Green is the green wet grass
The new leaves on trees in spring
The juicy ripe apples
Main colour of spring
The flowers waving in the wind

The salty seaweed
The silk inside the chestnut
The best colour ever
The colour of nature.

Liam Wheatley (10)
Shotton Hall Junior School

AUTUMN

Autumn is a conker inside its coat.
The dark of people at Hallowe'en.
Autumn is leaves falling off trees.
Big black and red fireworks.
The farmers gathering the harvest.
Autumn is people in thick coats.
Autumn is animals getting food before hibernation.
Autumn is birds flying here and there.
Autumn is grass when it is jewelled.

Lee Cuthbert (10)
Shotton Hall Junior School

AUTUMN IS . . .

Red sun dying down
Green crackling leaves beneath your feet
Brown, the crops in the field
Yellow, children playing by the mill
Gold birds flying to Africa
Orange animals hibernating in the cold
Autumn is great!

Jennifer Legg (10)
Shotton Hall Junior School

RED IS . . .

A colour that stands out most,
A rose sitting in the garden,
A colour that gives you a warning,
A colour in the sky on a morning.

A colour that runs around inside you,
A colour that drives you wild,
A colour in the poppy fields in summer,
Even the colour of our school jumper.

Kate Fletcher (10)
Shotton Hall Junior School